G000097520

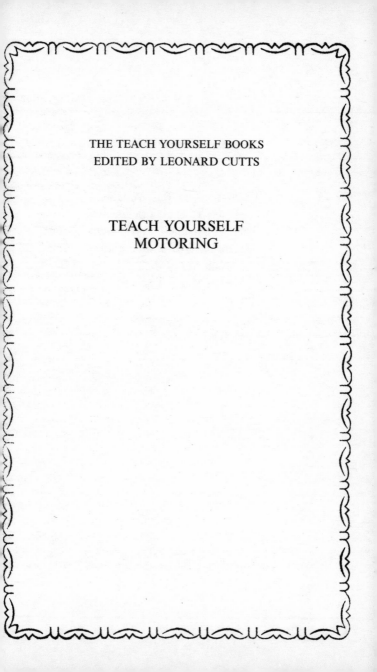

THE TEACH YOURSELF BOOKS
EDITED BY LEONARD CUTTS

TEACH YOURSELF
MOTORING

In the same series

———

Teach Yourself Bird Watching
Teach Yourself Cycling
Teach Yourself Good Manners
Teach Yourself Mothercraft
Teach Yourself to Fly
Teach Yourself to Live

Teach ®
Yourself

TEACH YOURSELF
MOTORING

By
DUDLEY NOBLE

PREFACE

THE motor vehicle is, to-day, essentially a part of everyone's normal life. Even if you do not own a car, you probably travel quite often in that of a friend, or, at any rate, in a coach or hired car, while not an inhabitant of the British Isles but must use public service motor vehicles to a greater or lesser extent.

We have certainly become a road-minded nation, and realise how much our daily lives are influenced by the motor vehicle. There is good reason to believe that the majority of Britain's population would like to possess a car of their own, and one cannot doubt that the number of cars in use is going to increase steadily as the years pass.

Many people who have never yet owned, or even driven, a car are likely to become motorists in the more or less near future, and it is, therefore, a good thing to learn as much as possible beforehand regarding driving and general maintenance, and also about the manner in which a motor car functions.

The purpose of this "Teach Yourself" book is to explain, as clearly and simply as possible, all that a motorist (or potential motorist) should know about a car and its use on the King's Highway. It is hoped that it will form a valuable preparation for the course of practical instruction that every novice must go through in order to qualify for a driving licence, and thereafter to be a safe and accident-free motorist.

Many an inexperienced motorist has allowed his car to suffer unnecessary harm because he failed to appreciate in good time that a certain amount of attention was demanded.

It is very desirable to acquire even a superficial knowledge
of the internal workings of a motor car in order to be able
to drive with sympathetic understanding, and, if the novice
who reads this book does secure a grasp of the whys and
wherefores to an extent that will spare him expense for
unnecessary repairs, the author will consider that his work
has served a useful purpose.

SUMMARY OF CONTENTS

Part I.—Driving

The requirements to be a good driver—The controls of a motor car—How a car steers—How the clutch works—The art of using the brakes—The accelerator and throttle—How to handle the gearbox—Pre-selector gearboxes—Synchro-mesh and what it means to the driver—Double-declutching explained—The choke and how to avoid damage to the engine in its use—Electrical controls and their operation—Trafficators.

Teaching oneself the handling of the car's controls—Starting up the engine and moving away—When to change gear—Making proper use of the brakes—Technique of driving round bends—When driving on icy roads how to keep control—Causation of accidents—Highway Code and road sense—Priority and consideration for other road users —Proper employment of the horn—Ethics of giving signals from the driving seat—The officially recognised hand signals—The mechanical traffic signal—Road signs and warnings—The " No Entry " sign—The " Halt " sign—The " Slow—Major Road Ahead " sign—Pedestrian crossings and the right method of approach to them—How a good driver behaves when at the wheel, when stopping his car, and when starting away—Headlamps and how to prevent them dazzling other drivers.

Part II.—" The Works " of a Motor Car

Descriptions of the general construction and method of operation of the petrol engine—The carburettor—The valves—The Otto or four-stroke principle—The two-stroke principle—The principle of the Diesel engine—The gas turbine's principle—The ignition system—The lubrication system—The cooling system—How all the components work in together.

Advancing the spark—The reason for "knocking"—How the valves are timed—The exhaust system and how a car is silenced—How the cooling water is circulated through the engine—The fan—Some observations about oil and an engine's demands upon it—The oil filters and pressure gauge—When oil pressure falls, the reason and remedy.

Component parts of the car's electrical system—The battery and its functions—The dynamo and what it does—The ampere meter—The ignition warning light—The fuses—The starter motor and what happens when you press the starter button—Hints about getting the best out of the electrical equipment—The sparking plugs and reasons for different " reaches " of the points.

How the engine's power is transmitted to the road wheels —The friction coupling, or clutch—The fluid flywheel, or hydraulic clutch—The normal type of gearbox—The pre-selector, or epicyclic, gearbox—The propeller shaft—The universal joints—The back axle final drive ratio—The differential gear and how it functions—The reverse gear—The freewheel and some hints on " coasting."

The suspension of a car on its axles—Semi-elliptic springing—Independent suspension, its advantages and types—Torsion bar suspension—Shock absorbers and the reason for them—Four-wheel brakes and some points to know about their action—Servo assistance for the brakes—Hydraulic braking—The handbrake—How steering effort is transmitted to the wheels—The track rod and ill-effects of maladjustment—Tyres and how to obtain maximum life from them—" Cornering power " of tyres—Evils of under-inflation.

Part III.—Maintenance of a Motor Car

Roadside troubles and how to diagnose their cause—points to check over when the engine stops—Summary of reasons for the engine failing to run—Distinguishing faults in the petrol system from those in the electrical equipment—Points to attend to every week or few hundred miles—How water may leak away from the radiator—Where frost may nip the water circulation—Anti-frost precautions—Replenishing the engine sump with oil—The value of upper cylinder lubricants—Use of additives in engine sump, gearbox and back axle—Use of a tyre gauge for maintenance of correct pressure—Changing wheels round—Attention to the battery—Brake adjustment—Cleaning out petrol system—Decarbonising engine—Cause of excessive oil consumption—Reboring cylinders—Virtues of chromium-plating in cylinders—Use of liners in cylinders to prolong life.

Part IV.—On the Road

Obtaining a driving licence—The driving test and points to know—Insurance matters—The motoring organisations and their functions.

A*

The author wishes to point out that the illustrations in this book have been drawn purely diagrammatically in order to convey their meaning in the simplest possible manner.

PART I

DRIVING

Is a good driver born or made? Controversy has raged about this ever since I, personally, became interested in mechanically-propelled vehicles nearly forty-five years ago.

Doubtless the question dates back much farther than that, but, whenever its origin may have been, it is safe to say that the opinion, in case of accident, was always that the other fellow was to blame. We—and, by " we," I mean all of us who drive motor cars to-day—are convinced that the manner in which we conduct ourselves at the wheel is exemplary.

Perhaps the safest answer to the " born or made " query is that a person whose nature and mentality conduce to a sense of responsibility and consideration for others should be readily trainable as a first-class driver. And, when I talk of such, I do not mean he who goes places in the fastest time, for to travel at a high average speed is not necessarily a criterion of good driving, as some people seem to think. Nor, by the same token, is the " crawler " bound to be a first-class driver.

To qualify for that enviable appellation, in my opinion, a person must emerge with credit from a number of tests, not every one of which is concerned with the time the car is actually in motion. But the underlying keynote of them all is consideration for others, apart, of course, from the sheerly technical matters of controlling the car's speed and direction. There are, in other words, two aspects to first-class driving, the technical and the ethical. Let us consider them under these headings, separately, for the moment.

The Technics of Driving

Sitting in the driving seat, we find the following controls, all of which should be easily and comfortably accessible. (It is highly important that they should be, a fact that is

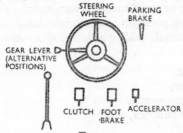

FIG. 1
The five primary controls of an average car.

recognised by car manufacturers to the extent that they make the driving seat adjustable, forwards and backwards, and also, in some cases, for height and angle. It cannot be too strongly emphasised that a driver should be thoroughly " at home " at the wheel, with the maximum of vision to the front and sides, while the rear-view mirror should be positioned so that the road behind is under observation for a distance of one hundred yards at least.)

A Car's Controls

1.—Steering wheel.
2.—Clutch pedal.
3.—Brake pedal.
4.—Accelerator pedal.
5.—Gear lever.

The foregoing are the five primary controls, in that they are the essential ones in guiding the car and regulating its speed. It is possible that, if this book is revised in ten years' time, the number of essential controls will have been reduced to three, since the advent of new types of transmission may abolish the need for a clutch pedal and a gear lever. For the moment, however, the vast majority of cars have the five essential controls enumerated. I will describe them in detail presently ; meanwhile, let us make a list of the other controls with which a driver must be familiar. They are :—

> Choke,
> Starter,
> Ignition switch,
> Light switches,
> Horn,
> Screen wiper,
> Direction indicators.

> Incidental controls comprise :—

> Radio,
> Heater and de-mister,
> Seat adjustment,
> Jacking system.

Let me describe the object and operation of each control in turn.

First, the steering wheel imparts guiding movement to the front wheels, which are mounted on swivelling spindles constructed integrally with what are called " king-pins." These work in bearings at top and bottom in a more or less upright plane. A rotating movement given to the steering wheel is transmitted via the steering column to a steering gearbox at its lower end, which is usually under the bonnet.

The steering gearbox converts the turning movement to pull and push, which is conveyed to an arm formed in one piece on the near- or off-side king-pin by means of a rod. As the steering wheel is turned, therefore, the king-pin causes the swivel arm to move, and carry the front wheel with it. On the other side of the car, the movement is transmitted by a coupling bar called the track rod so that the two front wheels move simultaneously.

Although the two wheels move whenever the steering wheel is turned, they do not stay exactly parallel. The reason for this is easily to be seen when it is realised that,

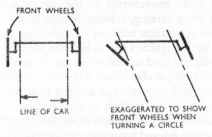

FRONT WHEELS

LINE OF CAR

EXAGGERATED TO SHOW FRONT WHEELS WHEN TURNING A CIRCLE

FIG. 2

The front wheels do not remain exactly parallel when the steering is locked over in turning a corner.

in turning a corner, the wheel on the inside of the curve is turning on a circle of smaller diameter than the outside wheel, and accordingly must be set at an angle compatible with that smaller circle. This is arranged automatically by the designer of the steering gear.

There are various forms of mechanism in the steering gearbox. One consists of a worm and nut, the worm being formed on the steering column, and the nut being forced to run up or down the column as the wheel is turned, thus setting up the pull-and-push motion. A rack and pinion is also employed for the same purpose, while a roller working in a spiral groove is another form of gear. The primary requirement is that the steering gear should be easy for the driver to manipulate, that it should never " stick " in one position but should be thoroughly free at every point in its movement. It should not allow road shocks from the front wheels to be transmitted to the driver's hands, at any rate to a considerable extent. The gear should be sufficiently high to enable the car to be fully controllable at high speeds without excessive movement of the steering wheel, and low enough to make manœuvring of the car in and out of garages, or when parking, reasonably light work.

A method sometimes used for immobilising cars, when parked, is for the ignition key to lock the steering column. Although this is a good scheme when the car is left standing in a street, it is not so convenient if the car is left in a public garage, when it is impossible to move it from one position to another unless the ignition is switched on. There is then a tendency for the ignition to be left on, which will run the battery down and may injure the ignition equipment.

The **Clutch** is a coupling between the engine and the transmission (whereby the engine's power is transmitted to the road wheels). When the clutch is " out " (that is, when the driver has pressed the clutch pedal down) there is no friction between the component parts comprising the clutch, because the springs which normally provide the friction between the clutch plates have been compressed. When the driver removes his foot from the clutch pedal, the effect is to allow the springs to come into play. " Slipping the clutch," therefore, means letting the clutch plates slide on each other by reducing the spring tension which otherwise binds them solidly together.

You can easily understand the action of the clutch if you imagine one of the clutch plates to be fixed to the engine shaft and the other to the propeller shaft which drives the back wheels of the car. When there is no friction between

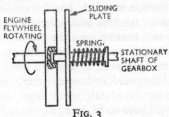

FIG. 3

The clutch causes the engine's rotation to be transmitted to the gear-box and road wheels by friction between two flat smooth surfaces.

the plates, the engine may revolve without its motion being transmitted to the road wheels. When, however, the driver eases his foot on the clutch pedal and allows the plates to " bite," the engine's power is directed towards turning the propeller shaft. The amount of " bite " is, of course, regulated by the degree of friction generated between the clutch plates by the springs ; the more gradually the driver " lets in " the clutch, as the operation is termed, the slower will be the rate of engagement, and the more gently the car will start into motion. Every clutch has its own " feel," and a driver must get to know each one's individuality. On some cars an infinitesimal movement of the clutch pedal may be all that is needed to let the clutch in fully ; on others the travel of the pedal to complete the operation may be considerable. Once a driver becomes proficient, he will be able to " feel " a clutch almost automatically, and to handle different cars readily after a preliminary try-out of the clutch.

To drive with the foot resting on the clutch pedal is bad

practice, for it is detrimental to the mechanism, causing heating up and undue wear of the bearings. Pressure on the clutch pedal, even quite light pressure, may set up clutch slip which can only be cured by dismantling and re-lining the plates with friction material. For this purpose, a special fabric which has an asbestos base is usually employed, and excessive wear and heating give the surface a glaze that prevents the clutch operating satisfactorily. Whenever there is no immediate need to use the clutch, therefore, keep the foot off the pedal, and never, *never*, " coast " down a hill by pressing the clutch pedal down—this is sheer cruelty, which will have to be cured expensively.

The **Brakes** are obvious in their purpose, but there is nevertheless an art in using them. In the hands (or under the feet) of some drivers they will need adjustment and renovation in half the time that our " first-class " driver will make them last in full efficiency, and will develop squeaks into the bargain.

The reason is that the best types of drivers confine the use of their brakes to an absolute minimum : they develop the knack of foretelling the need for speed reduction and arranging for it in ample time by allowing the engine to act as a brake prior to reaching the point where a slow speed, or a stop, will be required. On the other hand, a not-so-good driver will dash up to a corner and brake hard in the act of going round it. He is also prone to jam on his foot-brake at the slightest provocation, when a more " under-standing " driver would realise instinctively that a slowing down on the engine only would be sufficient.

To amplify the term just used, when the throttle is closed off by letting the accelerator pedal come up, the force required to rotate the " dead " engine is considerable, and the effect is to slow the car in marked fashion, even with top gear engaged. When descending a long and steep hill, to change down to third or second gear is sufficient to hold the car in check, making it necessary to apply the brakes in sparing fashion. This is important to remember when motoring in hilly or mountainous districts, since undue use of the brakes is not only conducive to excessive wear, but can make them lose power, due to the heat developed by the friction of the brake shoes in the wheel drums.

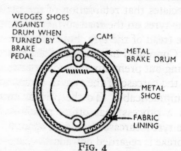

FIG. 4

A car's brakes usually consist of shoes lined with friction material which are caused to expand inside a metal drum when the brake pedal is pressed.

Brake shoes, like clutch plates, are lined with a fabric of non-combustible nature, but, at the same time, the effect of great heat is harmful in that the surface loses its gripping power, and the brakes " fade " into impotence. This is a most unpleasant matter for the driver on a long and twisty descent, and the only remedy is to stop when opportunity permits and allow the brakes to cool off, when they regain their power, although they may later have to be adjusted to compensate for wear of the linings. Under similar circumstances, a good driver would have let the engine perform most of the retarding effort, saving his brakes for occasional use at specially dangerous points.

I said just now that brake linings were made of non-combustible material, yet it has been known for brakes to catch fire. The reason for this would be that oil has leaked on to the brake linings, from axle or bearings, and intense heat generated by excessive use of the brakes has ignited it —the oil, not the lining.

The first-class driver will use his brakes to the least possible extent, not alone to save wear on them, but because he also appreciates that retardation of the car is caused by the grip of the tyres on the road surface. And this does not mean just the tread of the tyre, but the whole casing of the outer cover. Continued hard usage of the brakes will result in tyres wearing out prematurely, and, in extreme instances, may damage the carcase of the tyre to an extent that makes re-treading impracticable. To the private owner of a car, retreading is a process that offers much economy, and, therefore, the tyre's carcase should be spared.

The handbrake is regarded nowadays, generally speaking, as a parking brake, to hold the car at a standstill when left standing. Often it is designed to act on the rear wheels only, and is applied by direct mechanical connection with the brake lever, whereas the footbrake brings the majority of its power to bear on the front wheels, and often has hydraulic and other devices which amplify the effort exerted by the driver.

The **Accelerator** is the control which opens and closes the throttle, so admitting more or less gas to the engine and causing it to run faster or slower. The throttle itself is a valve in the inlet pipe, through which the engine draws the gaseous explosive mixture, which has been prepared by the carburettor from petrol and air. The accelerator pedal is spring-loaded, and, when foot pressure is relaxed, it allows the throttle valve to close off until it reaches a pre-arranged stop, set to permit only sufficient mixture to pass to enable the engine to run slowly, or " tick over," as it is called.

In driving a car, the right foot is kept permanently on the accelerator pedal (except when required to operate the foot-brake), and variation in the car's speed is obtained by giving more or less pressure on this pedal. In the use of this con-

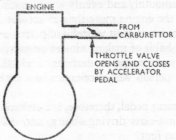

FIG. 5

The throttle valve in the pipe admitting explosive gas to the engine enables the amount of the charge to be regulated by the driver.

trol there is, again, great scope for the exercise of driving ability, and one person will extract more miles from the gallon of petrol than another merely by his superior skill in using the accelerator.

The basic reason for this lies in the fact that an engine works most economically when running at as nearly as possible a constant rate of revolution, at what is known as its " critical " speed. The latter is an intangible quantity, which a driver senses instinctively once he has gained experience. It is, briefly, the speed at which the engine is found to run most willingly and sweetly ; it varies, of course, with almost every car, and is normally found in the 30 to 40 m.p.h. range. Perhaps I may best describe it as being the speed at which the engine seems to *want* to run.

Naturally, one cannot always drive a car at the engine's critical speed, but it certainly helps consumption if the car is given as much running as is conveniently possible at this speed. In any case, the good driver will always aim to avoid frequent changes, or perhaps I should say abrupt changes, of engine speed. He will not jab on the accelerator, but will press it smoothly and evenly when gaining speed, and will not race the engine more than is absolutely necessary. Sharp acceleration is most wasteful of petrol, and the driver who is in the habit of making violent getaways from traffic lights or wayside stops is deriving less value from his petrol than a person who accelerates in a calm, unhurried manner.

The accelerator pedal, therefore, is a control which enters largely into first-class driving ability, and calls for use by brain as well as foot.

The **Gear Lever** controls the gearbox, which is an essential part of a motor car because of the inherent disability of a motor car's engine to develop any real amount of power unless running at a fairly high rate of speed. This is where it differs fundamentally from a steam engine, which starts itself off from a standstill and pulls with as much vigour at low speeds as high.

Every power unit of the " internal combustion " type, which description covers all engines using petrol or fuel oil to be ignited inside the cylinder, such as every motor car employs, has to revolve at a certain rate of speed in order to produce power efficiently. If, for example, it requires 5 h.p. to put a car into motion from rest, then the throttle must be opened until the engine is revolving at a speed where it develops about that amount of power. An engine's horse-power potentiality is described as being so many h.p. " on brake test " (b.h.p.) at so many revolutions per minute. This test is carried out on a special testing bed, with the engine coupled up to a variable brake, or power absorber, which can be adjusted to consume any amount of power while the engine is running. The maximum reading is usually obtained at a speed in the region of 4,000 r.p.m., which would correspond, with the car in top gear on the road, to

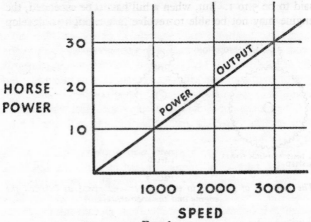

FIG. 6

The rising line indicates how the power of an engine goes up as its rate of revolution increases (actual power varies with size of engine).

perhaps 60 m.p.h. At lower rates of revolution, the engine gives off disproportionately less power, so that, at a few hundred r.p.m., it would be incapable of driving the car, except perhaps on a level road.

It is accordingly necessary to have some means of co-ordinating engine speed and road wheel speed so that the power output of the motor is adequate to the load it has to pull. On a level road the load will be lighter than when climbing a hill, and that 5 h.p. I mentioned as being the power necessary to start the car from rest may be sufficient, once in motion along a level road, to drive it at 20 m.p.h. on top gear.

On that gear, the engine may be revolving five times to every one turn of the road wheels (the exact ratio varies with different cars) ; in other words, top gear ratio would be said to be 5 to 1. But, when a hill has to be ascended, the engine may not be able to revolve fast enough to develop

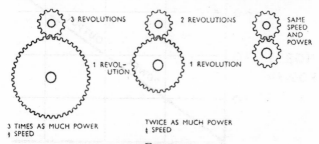

FIG. 7

The function of gears is to vary power and speed as between the engine and the road wheels.

sufficient power to pull the increased load, and, once its " revs " fall, so does its power. A device is thus needed whereby the ratio between engine and road wheels may be increased, and this is exactly what the gearbox does.

Inside the gearbox there are several pairs of gear wheels, each pair having different ratios of size by comparison one with another. On one pair, for example, the small wheel may have ten teeth and the large wheel fifteen ; the former will therefore revolve one and a half times to every revolution of the other. Another pair may have a two-to-one ratio, and so on. If the engine's power can be transmitted through any pair of gear wheels, at choice, it will be obvious that the ratio between the engine and the road wheels may be varied to the extent provided by the gearbox.

Three or four forward gear ratios are provided on a car, plus one reverse : the latter is always a very low ratio gear. For the major part of its time on the road, the car runs on top gear, where there is a " direct drive " from the engine,

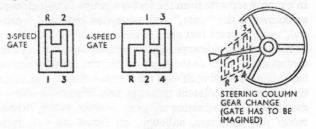

3-SPEED GATE

4-SPEED GATE

STEERING COLUMN GEAR CHANGE (GATE HAS TO BE IMAGINED)

FIG. 8

The " gate " of the gearbox is sometimes invisible to the driver, but the diagrams show how it controls the path of the gear lever from one position to another, with intermediate " neutral " position.

through the clutch and the gearbox to the final transmission inside the back axle. Here the ratio between the directly-driven propeller shaft and the road wheels is set (usually—see footnote)* at a constant figure, which may be anything between 3 to 1 and 5 to 1. This means that, even in top gear, the engine is always revolving that number of times to one turn of the road wheels. The exact ratio is set by the car's designer, and takes into consideration many factors which vary with different models, such as size of tyres, the power-to-weight ratio of the car, also its intended top speed. Sometimes this ratio is varied according to the market or district into which the car is originally delivered. At all

* A two-speed rear axle has been tried, but is seldom employed on private cars.

events, the final drive ratio is fixed and unalterable, and does not concern the gearbox.

The gear lever brings into operation, at the will of the driver, any one of the three or four forward speeds, or reverse, depending on the position in which he sets it. In the case of a four-speed gearbox, reverse position is located in a groove separate from the forward gears. These grooves are known as the " gate," and, when the lever is in " neutral," which means that none of the gears is engaged, it can be moved freely sideways. Each gear position leads off this central gate, either to the front or the rear, and the driver has to familiarise himself with the location of each gear, since this varies with different makes of car. There is, unfortunately, no standardisation of gear position among British motor manufacturers, although, on American cars, it is recognised that reverse and first gears shall be opposite one another, likewise second and top on the far side of the gate.

The gear-change lever may protrude from the floor of the driving compartment, or it may be on the steering column. The latter position was adopted on some of the very earliest cars, and history is now repeating itself, since many post-war models have it in the same location. It is important to bear in mind, however, that, wherever the gear lever may be placed, the gate type of change, already explained, is used on all gearboxes of what may best be described as the " normal " pattern, and by this I mean the kind found on the majority of cars, which nowadays are referred to as being " synchro-mesh."

With this type of gearbox, the procedure is to engage each gear after having pressed the clutch pedal. It is necessary to free the clutch because the action of engaging a gear is only possible when the driving force of the engine is relieved.

By pressing out the clutch, and, at the same time, releasing the accelerator pedal so that the engine does not race away once the load is relaxed, it becomes possible to move the gear lever from one position to another. This action causes different pairs of gear wheels, of varying size, to be engaged, and, when the operation is completed by once more allowing the clutch to return " home," the engine is connected to the driving wheels of the car through the medium of the desired gear.

If the car should be fitted with a gearbox of the type known as " pre-selector," or " automatic change " (these are the alternatives to that which I have termed " normal "), the procedure varies because the movement of the gear lever does not directly bring about the changing of the gears. The lever pre-selects the gear which is next to be engaged, but the operation itself is performed by pressing down, and immediately releasing, the pedal which would compare to the clutch pedal on a normal car. On vehicles which are equipped with a pre-selector gearbox, however, this is not an ordinary clutch and is usually supplemented by a fluid flywheel, or automatic clutch, which provides the same purpose as the normal clutch, namely a friction coupling between engine and transmission.

As has already been pointed out, the motor car engine develops its fullest power when running at a fairly high speed—not necessarily its very highest—so that, when an uphill gradient causes the car's speed to flag, it may be essential to change to a lower gear in order to prevent it stalling. As to when a change down is required, experience will soon tell. Sometimes, of course, it will be forced on a driver that he *must* change ; at others, it may be doubtful (even to an old hand) whether or not he should change. All that can be said is that a first-class driver will not let his engine labour unnecessarily, nor will he race it unreasonably.

A driver will get to know, as he gains experience with his car, the effectiveness of each gear ratio. If there are four speeds, there will be less of a gap between each than in the case of a three-speed car. A good plan is to watch the speedometer dial and note how fast the engine is " revving " at the various road speeds. For example, on first gear, the engine will be running quite fast when the car is travelling at no more than about ten or twelve m.p.h. On second, the car may do anything between twenty and forty m.p.h., depending on whether there are three or four speeds in the gearbox. If there are four, second gear will naturally be lower than if there are only three, while third will be sufficiently high to enable the car to travel at, perhaps, forty to sixty m.p.h., according to the power of the engine.

This does not mean to imply that one should always use one of the intermediate gears until the car has attained the speed indicated. In ordinary circumstances, top gear would be used, once under way, and irrespective of the number of intermediate gears, at all speeds after attaining about twenty m.p.h., and the car will probably idle along, still on top, at speeds down to ten m.p.h., or even less. But, in climbing a hill, it is useful to know whether one will find it advantageous to change down at, say, thirty m.p.h., or whether to allow the car to slow down still further before engaging a lower gear. So much depends on the length of the hill and the local conditions that it is impossible to lay down a hard and fast rule. If the driver senses that it *will* be necessary to change down, however, he will not leave it too late before making the change, otherwise he will have lost way and the engine may fail to sustain the load, even on the next lower ratio, and a further change down may be required. Again, sometimes it may be possible to increase the car's speed by changing down, even though the engine is capable of driving the car up the hill on top gear without undue labouring, because the engine will run faster. The choice, in such case, must be left to the individual driver, and experience with the actual car involved alone can guide him in his actions.

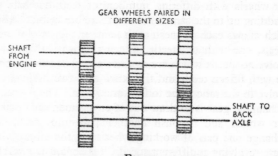

GEAR WHEELS PAIRED IN DIFFERENT SIZES

SHAFT FROM ENGINE

SHAFT TO BACK AXLE

FIG. 9
Three pairs of gear wheels which indicate how one shaft can turn another at varying speeds while remaining a fixed distance apart.

The modern types of gearbox, with their "synchromesh," or simplified change speed, also "pre-selector" patterns, have largely robbed driving of one of its greatest terrors for the novice. There was a time when it was essential to master the intricacies of what is known as "double-declutching" in order to make a change down without a horrid clashing of gears. Perhaps a few notes should be given on this subject, in case any reader should have to learn to drive on a car of old, or synchromesh-less, type.

To understand the need for double-declutching, it is desirable to have an idea as to the interior workings of a gearbox. Let us therefore imagine an "input" shaft,

driven by the engine, and an " output " shaft, driving the
rear wheels of the car. The two shafts revolve at the same
speed when top gear is engaged, but at varying speeds on
the intermediate gears, and the slower the output shaft
revolves by comparison with the input shaft, the lower is
the gear ratio in use.

These varying speeds are arranged by providing pairs of
gear wheels with differing numbers of teeth on each, yet
all adding up to the same total and therefore being of a size
which allows each to mesh with another. A pair of gear
wheels, one with ten teeth and another with thirty, will
revolve at speeds which are as three to one : another pair,
one with fifteen teeth and the other with twenty-five, will
revolve in the ratio three to five, and so on. The operation
of changing gear is to draw out of engagement one pair of
gear wheels and to push another pair into mesh. To
exchange one pair of working wheels for the other, while
all are revolving at different speeds, it is obviously desirable
to endeavour to bring the pair about to be meshed into as
close a harmony as possible, or a clashing of teeth will be
caused which will not only sound harsh but will be detrimental to them, no matter how strong and well hardened
they may be.*

Double-declutching is an operation which speeds up the
slower-running of the gear wheels about to be engaged
when changing to a lower gear. To perform it, the clutch
pedal is pressed and the gear lever simultaneously moved
to neutral ; the clutch is let in for a brief moment and,
at the same instant, the accelerator is pressed, speeding up
the engine and, with it, the slower-running gear wheel ;

---

* Although the principle is similar, most modern gearboxes have
gears which are in constant mesh, and only the " dog clutches "
revolve at varying speeds.

the clutch pedal is next pressed out again and the gear lever "snicked" into the lower ratio notch, and, lastly, the clutch is let in again.

The average touring car of to-day is so provided for in its gearbox that double-declutching is unnecessary. Synchro-mesh, as its name implies, is a method whereby the meshing gear wheels are synchronised in speed, the operation being performed by a pair of friction rings,

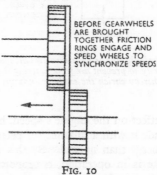

BEFORE GEARWHEELS ARE BROUGHT TOGETHER FRICTION RINGS ENGAGE AND SPEED WHEELS TO SYNCHRONIZE SPEEDS

FIG. 10

The principle of synchro-mesh is to synchronise the speeds of gear wheels before they are brought into mesh.

which come into contact immediately before the gears are meshed, and thereby achieve the same result as double-declutching. It is, however, important to bear in mind that the movement of the gear lever, with synchro-mesh, should be deliberate in order to allow of synchronisation being effective.

We have now taken stock of the five major controls of a motor car, which the driver will be handling throughout the whole time he is in command of the wheel. There are, however, the various ancillary controls enumerated at the outset with which he must be equally familiar, and we will, therefore, proceed to survey them and ascertain their various uses.

The **Choke** must not be confused with the throttle, although both are concerned with the carburettor. The

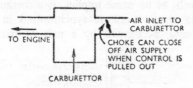

FIG. 11

Although the choke looks like another throttle valve, and acts similarly, its function is merely to prevent air from entering the carburettor and thereby enrich the explosive mixture.

choke has no effect on the engine's speed, but is merely a device to provide it with a mixture (of petrol gas and air) which is " richer " than normal. By this is meant that, when the choke is in operation, a proportion of the air which would otherwise be drawn in through the carburettor is choked off, thus making the mixture which passes into the cylinder of the engine richer in petrol gas. This is necessary to give the easiest possible starting up, and to assist the engine to develop a reasonable amount of power before it attains its proper working temperature.

The choke can, however, be very harmful to the engine if it is left in operation even a moment longer than is absolutely necessary. By reason of it causing a mixture rich in petrol vapour to enter the cylinders, some of the essential lubricating oil which coats their walls is dissolved away, with results that will show themselves in the after-life of the engine. Undue wear of the cylinders may necessitate them being rebored far earlier than would otherwise be the case.

The choke control usually takes the form of a pull-out knob situated on the facia board, and the driver must take the greatest care to push it in again once the engine has settled down to normal running. It is best to let the engine run fairly fast, under a light load, after starting up, and not to keep it idling with the choke pulled right out. The object should be to induce a circulation of oil as soon as possible after starting, so that such oil as is washed off the cylinder walls by the rich mixture will be replaced without delay.

The **Starter** on most cars is electric, and is controlled by a push-in or pull-out knob, but sometimes there is a special type of actuation peculiar to the make concerned. One of the few things that the driver should know about an electric starter is that it draws a great deal of current from the battery, so that excessive use of the starter may discharge the battery abnormally. As long as the car's dynamo keeps up its recuperative work, and provided the car is driven for sufficiently long runs to enable the dynamo to replace the charge taken out of the battery, reasonable use of the starter is unlikely to prove harmful.

The **Ignition Switch** is a control of which the purpose is immediately obvious. Usually a detachable key is provided, and often it is arranged that various other controls become inoperative once the ignition has been switched off —trafficators and screen wipers, for instance. A red light glowing on the dash is the normal indication provided to warn the driver that the ignition is turned on ; this light extinguishes itself once the charging current from the dynamo attains sufficient strength to take the ignition's drain off the battery. When stationary, or at very slow speeds, the current required for the ignition is drawn from

the battery, which would run itself down if the car were left
standing for a considerable time with the ignition switched
on and engine dead ; damage might also be done to the
ignition equipment itself.

A car's **Lights** are turned on or off by a switch on the
facia board, in the general way, although it is the practice

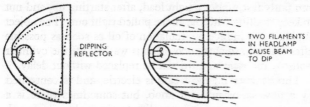

DIPPING
REFLECTOR

TWO FILAMENTS
IN HEADLAMP
CAUSE BEAM
TO DIP

FIG. 12

*Two methods of dipping the headlamps' beam—one mechanical and
the other electrical.*

of certain foreign makers to place the control on an arm
beneath the steering wheel. There are normally three
positions for the switch—off, side and head. The first
movement of the switch causes the side and tail lamps to
light, and the second brings on the headlamps in addition.
A separate control, either foot or hand operated, dims or
dips the headlamps, this operation being effected either by
a movement of the reflector of the nearside headlamp, the
offside lamp being extinguished automatically at the same
moment*, or by the use of two separate filaments inside the
headlamp bulbs, which produce the same dipping effect.

Nowadays, when so many cars have their front lamps
encased in the wings, it is not possible for the driver to keep
his sidelamps under observation from the driving seat.
It is, therefore, generally arranged that the light illumina-
ting the facia board and instruments (called the panel

* The latest practice is for both headlamps to dip their beam.

B

light) will only come on when the sidelamps have been switched on.

The **Screen Wipers** on most British cars are worked electrically, or by a drive from the engine, although many American makers still adhere to vacuum-operation from the engine. They may be positioned at the top or bottom of the windscreen, and, if the screen is of the pattern that opens, it is usual for the wiper control to have a sliding spindle which, when pushed forward, lifts the wiper blade over the edge of the ridge of the screen, on which it would otherwise stick. When the screen is fixed, however, a single on-and-off switch is provided, the wiper-blade resting on the glass continually.

A screen wiper is effective when rain is actually falling, but, when the roads are wet and the weather is dry, as happens in spring and autumn particularly, the screen becomes spattered with mud thrown up by other vehicles. Water squirted from a small reservoir carried on the car is needed to counteract this, and such devices are now often fitted to cars. Operated either by vacuum from the engine, or by a manual pump with control from the facia board, water is ejected through a tiny nozzle on to the windscreen in the path of the wiper blade.

Direction Indicators (Trafficators) have advantages as compared with the old method of extending an arm in order to signify intention of turning. They also have disadvantages, such as failure to cancel themselves under certain conditions, and it is no uncommon thing to see a car proceeding along a straight road with the indicator out. A good driver will assure himself that his indicator has cancelled itself after making a turn, as it is very confusing to following vehicles for unintentional signals to be given.

Traffic indicators employed on some foreign makes of

car are of the flashing-light type (known as " clignoteur "). Lamps at front and rear of a car, generally yellow or orange, are caused to light up intermittently on the side of the car towards which a turn is to be made.

The control for trafficators usually takes the form of a small lever, situated on the steering wheel or on the facia board, which the driver moves in the direction towards which the turn is to be made. Cancellation is often effected automatically by a concealed ratchet inside the steering column, actuated by the motion of straightening up the wheel. Sometimes a time switch is provided, which cancels the signal after allowing it to show for a certain space of time, while manual control is fitted on some cars, with a red light which shows whenever the signal arm is extended.

The remainder of the controls, such as horn, radio, heater and de-mister, seat adjustment and jacking system, call for no special comment and amplification, as they are not germane to the driving of a car.

And so, having learned the nature and purpose of the various controls, let us proceed to teach ourselves to drive. Sitting in the driving seat, and with the engine dead, and cold, our first precaution would be to make sure that the gear lever was in neutral position.

We should then pull out the choke control,* turn on the ignition and press (or pull) the starter knob. Almost at once the engine should start up, and we should wait for a few moments until it settled down to steady running.

Up to now we have not pressed the accelerator pedal, for the action of pulling out the choke usually causes the throttle

---

* This applies to the general run of modern cars, except that, in some cases, the choke is automatically operated, being put in and out of action by thermostatic control. There is then no manual control.

to be opened slightly, the makers setting it in what they consider to be the best position for starting.

With the engine running, we now press the clutch pedal right down and slip the gear lever into first-speed position. If the car is on level ground, we take off the handbrake, speed up the engine a little by pressing gently on the accelerator, and at the same time let the clutch pedal come back against the pressure of our left foot until we feel the clutch " bite," and the car start to move.

All these motions should be gone through time and time again (without stopping the engine between each occasion, in order to spare the battery) until they are made instinctively, and can be performed without taking the eyes off the road ahead.

In the case of a car fitted with **Pre-selector Gearbox,** our procedure would be to start up the engine, first making sure the gear really was in neutral by pressing the " clutch " pedal to the floor with lever set in N position. We should then move the gear lever to first-speed position and again press the pedal, letting it come up again immediately. Now releasing the handbrake, and pressing the accelerator, the car would start to move forward, without any further manipulation of the " clutch " pedal.

To venture on the road, of course, we must have obtained our provisional driving licence, have fixed " L " plates to the car, and be accompanied by a qualified driver. (There is more about these matters at the end of the book.) Let me, therefore, go on further in what I may term a theoretical manner.

Once the car had moved off on bottom gear, we should soon find that the engine was running unduly fast in relation to the road speed of the car. This would indicate that a higher gear was required, and so we should decide to change up. We should press the clutch pedal with our left foot, and simultaneously ease our right foot from the accelerator to avoid the engine racing when the clutch was freed. We should now move the gear lever from first- to second-speed position, and, the instant it was home, we should let the clutch pedal come up smoothly but deliberately. At the same moment, we should press down gently on the accelerator.

We should now be travelling at a higher road speed than on first gear, but with the engine turning over more slowly, because of the higher gear ratio. Assuming that we were on a level road, we should soon find that another change up was called for, and should perform this as before. If the car were a three-speed type, we should now be in top gear; if it were a four-speed, yet another change would be needed, in similar fashion to the previous ones.

In the case of a **Pre-selector Gearbox,** the procedure would be to move the gear lever to the next position upwards, and then (but not simultaneously) to press down the " clutch " pedal and let it come up again smartly.

On top gear we should proceed until the time came for a change down to be made, when our motions would be exactly the same as before. If we were climbing a hill, we should want to lose as little way as possible, and hence we should not ease our foot off the accelerator quite so much as when changing up. The engine would be allowed to run faster, because, when the lower gear is engaged, the engine will have to speed up in order to carry the car along at the same, or nearly the same, road speed on the lower ratio.

As we became more used to driving, we should not press the clutch pedal quite so hard when changing down, as compared with changing up, but merely enough to free the friction surfaces of the clutch and enable the gear lever to be moved. This, of itself, would help the gear wheels to synchronise their speeds, as we saw was necessary when double-declutching. The basic principle to be borne in mind is that the engine must run faster in relation to the road wheels on the lower gear ratios, and must accordingly

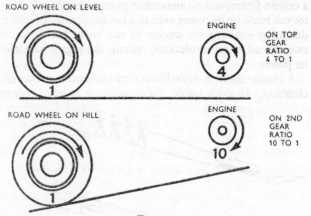

FIG. 13

The engine is allowed to run faster in relation to the road wheels when a lower gear is engaged for hill-climbing.

be speeded up—to catch up with the car, so to speak—when changing down.

I mentioned earlier that experience alone could tell a driver when he should change gear, especially down. Judgment in this matter quickly develops as a person gains knowledge of a car, and driving confidence increases. Briefly, one changes *up* when the engine seems to be carrying the load too easily on an intermediate gear, and changes *down* when the engine gives signs of undue labouring on an upgrade.

By " undue labouring " is meant the feeling of forcing against too heavy odds, the inability of the engine to respond to full throttle opening and a marked falling-off in its rate of revolution. As we have noted, a motor car engine suffers great loss of power when its rate of revolution drops below a certain figure, and no amount of pressure on the accelerator can build up its power once this has happened. A change down, by enabling the engine to run faster for the same rate of road wheel revolutions, permits the engine to regain its power.

A change down is desirable at times other than when hill climbing. In thick traffic, for instance, it is wise to drop

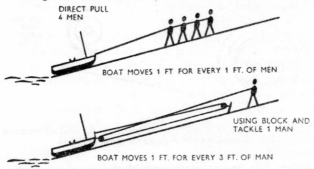

DIRECT PULL
4 MEN

BOAT MOVES 1 FT FOR EVERY 1 FT. OF MEN

USING BLOCK AND
TACKLE 1 MAN

BOAT MOVES 1 FT. FOR EVERY 3 FT. OF MAN

FIG. 14
A block and tackle used for hauling a boat up a beach is similar in principle to a car's gearbox.

into third or second gear so that the car will crawl behind slow-moving vehicles, yet be all ready to accelerate vigorously when an opening permits. On a lower gear the engine will be pulling a less load—a remark which may perhaps be amplified by saying that, although the weight of the car naturally does not vary, the load placed on the engine is less

on a lower gear, in the same way that men hauling a load—
say a boat up a beach—will find their work lightened if they
employ a block and tackle. This acts in similar fashion to
a gearbox on a car, because it transforms feet of movement
at the " input " end of the rope into inches at the " output "
end.

An engine with a flywheel one foot in diameter may be
said to " move " three feet at every revolution. If its gear
ratio in relation to the road wheels is five to one on top gear,
it will be " moving " fifteen feet to every one revolution of
the road wheels, which might be two feet in diameter and
therefore six feet (approx.) in circumference. The ratio
between engine and road wheel " movement " on top gear
would thus be fifteen to six : if, on a lower gear, the engine
revolves ten times for every revolution of the road wheels,
the ratio obviously falls to thirty to six, which, in the case
of our men with the block and tackle, would mean that they
pulled thirty feet of rope to haul their boat six feet up the
beach.

If I appear to labour this point of gearing it is because
the gearbox and all that appertains to it are the most
difficult points for a novice to grasp, but they are extremely
important to the driver of a car of British type, which usually
has an engine of small dimensions, at any rate by comparison
with an American car. With the latter, the gearbox is used,
in its intermediate ratios, to a far less extent, because its
large engine has a more ample margin of power, even at low
speeds. Furthermore, the American car generally has an
engine with six or more cylinders, whereas the average
British car (I refer to those of what may best be termed the
" popular " type) is powered by a four-cylinder unit. It is
a characteristic of a multi-cylinder engine that its " flexibility," or ability to run smoothly and develop power at low

speeds, is more marked than in the case of single-cylinder, two-cylinder or four-cylinder engines. The reason, of course, lies in the greater number of power strokes to each revolution of the flywheel.

The uses of the **Brakes** may seem obvious, but here, again, there is a technique in driving which requires a little special understanding to appreciate fully.

The brakes are employed not only to bring the car to a standstill, but also to check its speed. In approaching a

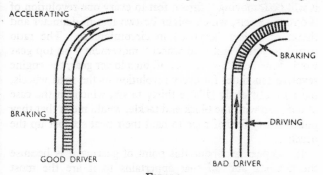

ACCELERATING

BRAKING

BRAKING

DRIVING

GOOD DRIVER

BAD DRIVER

FIG. 15

A good driver will slow his car before reaching a bend and then " drive " round it, instead of braking while actually on the bend.

bend, corner or danger spot, a good driver will make a gentle application of the footbrake in plenty of time before reaching the point where a reduced speed may be called for ; he will, in other words, have the car always " in hand."

If rounding a bend, the best driving technique is, after having slowed the car sufficiently on the straight approach, to accelerate as the car goes into the turn. This is an important point, and one that every new driver should master : never (except in emergency) apply the brakes when actually

B*

rounding a bend, but accelerate and *drive* the car round it.

The reason behind this advice is the action of the differential, of which we shall learn more at a later stage of this book. Let it be sufficient now to say that the differential is a system of gear wheels, built into the back axle, which permits the two road wheels that drive the car to rotate at different speeds, although they are apparently on the same axle shaft. The amount of differential movement

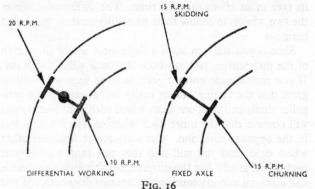

FIG. 16

A differential gear permits the two driving wheels to revolve at varying speeds when turning a corner.

allowed to the wheels is, however, controlled to the extent that the wheels are obliged to rotate at proportionately varying speeds when they are not going round together at the same speed. Should this sound a little complicated, let me try to explain by saying that, if one wheel goes faster than the other, then the latter must go at the same relative speed *slower* than if both were revolving at the driving speed of the car.

Look at it this way; when a car rounds a bend or corner the outside wheel has got a greater distance to travel than the inner one—think of the soldiers on parade when they " wheel " : the men on the outer flanks have to march in quick time while the pivot men are marking time. If there was no differential in the back axle of a car, and both wheels were firmly fixed at the opposite ends of a solid driving shaft, imagine what would happen. The outer wheel would be skidding in its hurry to get round, while the inner one would be churning the ground, wearing out its tyre in an effort to mark time. The differential allows the two wheels to follow their particular courses in perfect harmony.

Should you want to learn a little more about the action of the differential, jack up both the back wheels of a car. If you now engage bottom gear, so as to impose a load so great that the engine cannot easily be rotated by the propeller shaft, and turn one back wheel with your hands, you will observe that the other back wheel is also rotating, but in the opposite direction. Get someone to hold the other wheel rigid, and you will find that you cannot turn your back wheel at all. But the differential, although so valuable and essential to every touring car, has this drawback ; if you park your car on wet grass, or in snow, and one wheel has the chance to slip on the surface, it will spin round without driving the car, while the other wheel will remain placidly static. It is for this reason that racing cars either do not have differentials, or have types which can be locked solid, so that both wheels must always drive together at the same speed in the same direction.

Now, in *driving* the car round a bend, as I have just said is the right technique, the propeller shaft from the engine is actually helping the differential to do its job effectively. If, on the other hand, the brakes are applied, the compensating device, which is a feature of every braking system (with the object of equalising the pressure of brake shoes on the drums), is being thrown out of balance because the wheels are revolving at different speeds. The effect of this, especially if the road surface should be conducive to skids, may be embarrassing—or worse—to the driver. Always avoid, therefore, using the brakes on a corner or bend if you can possibly do so. Should the road surface be in any way " tricky," change down to a lower gear—*before* reaching the bend—rather than take the chance of relying on the brakes in case you have to use them.

Brakes can be dangerous things if they are not maintained in proper adjustment, especially the front-wheel brakes. A point often not appreciated to the full is that brakes which act powerfully, but without much " progressiveness," can be a real menace on skiddy surfaces. They are known as being " fierce " when in this state. Remember that, the instant a wheel locks because of excessive brake application, the friction between tyre and road surface breaks down, and the vehicle may go out of control. A fierce brake will always be tending to lock the wheels, whereas one that is more progressive in its action, even though not so apparently powerful, will apply more gradual retarding effect, and maintain that friction between wheel and road which is, after all, the sole method whereby a moving vehicle is brought to rest.

When driving on an ice-bound road, exercise the most intense care when braking, and use the gears instead of the brakes to apply retarding effort. Once the wheels lock, you may release pressure on the brake pedal altogether, and yet the friction between tyres and road will be insufficient to restart the wheels. In other words, the car will be out of control after one false move. A good tip, if only you can remember it at the exact moment, is to

" pump " the brake pedal rather than to press it down. A series of jabs will induce braking effect without giving the wheels time to lock. This procedure was recommended after tests of driving on a frozen lake by research workers in America. They also found that snow chains are useless on ice, because they cannot bite into a hard surface and, if fitted, wear out rapidly. Chains are helpful only in thick snow, and, for all other types of wintry road a good non-skid tread is best.

Tyres with steel studs used to be much employed, but they went out of favour because, as road surfaces improved and became waterproof, the steel studs were unsuitable for most types of roads and really suited only a few. Nowadays, there is a process of cutting thin slits in a tyre tread, which is helpful on greasy and icy surfaces, while a recently discovered method of embedding wire in the ribs of a tyre is perhaps the best anti-skid yet developed. The latter process is (at the time of writing) applicable only to retreaded tyres, but it certainly appears to be a very promising device.

It is an often-quoted axiom that accidents do not " happen," but are caused. The fundamental truth of this is apparent on reflection, but it is nevertheless usual, when told of how an accident " happened," to gain the impression that it was (as a learned judge once remarked after listening to both sides of a case) a collision between two stationary vehicles on opposite sides of the road.

The plain truth is, of course, that nearly every accident is *caused* through one driver taking just a bit of a chance at the exact moment that another driver is doing the same thing. For ninety-nine days out of a hundred the average man may be the most careful driver it is possible to imagine. On that one day in a hundred he takes a chance, and, if he is unlucky, he falls foul of another driver or pedestrian who is having *his* occasional lapse also.

How to guard against these infrequent lapses is one of the biggest problems of those who desire to see the accident rate reduced—and who does not ? A proportion are caused, not by habitually dangerous drivers, but by good, average drivers who happened to have a momentary defection from normal carefulness and were so unfortunate as to encounter at that instant someone else who was likewise off form.

It is easy, and customary, for anyone who writes about driving technique to point out that one should always take the greatest care when in control of a car. While I unhesitatingly follow suit, I would like to go further, and assert that the day will come when every person who reads these words will, while at the wheel, pull himself up with a start and exclaim, in his inner consciousness, " I took a risk then. Thank heaven it was my lucky day and I didn't meet somebody else who was taking a risk too." I hope it *will* be a lucky day, and I hope, also, that a mental and very sincere resolve will be made, on the spot, that there is going to be one hundred per cent. attention to driving in the future.

Now, I am quite prepared to admit that some accidents are due to inexperience, and, perhaps, ignorance, rather than to carelessness or inattention. Let me at least, therefore, run through the more obvious points from which trouble arises on the road.

In the first place, the Highway Code ought to be read understandingly ; not just in superficial manner so that questions concerning it can be answered parrot fashion. The Highway Code is a very sane and common-sense manual to proper behaviour when using the road, and the purport of its instruction, permanently carried into practice, would rob the roads of a large proportion of their present danger. I will assume that every person who uses the road, either as driver or pedestrian, has done his duty and familiarised himself with the Highway Code. Let us proceed to an amplification of its advice, with special reference to what the learner-driver ought to get into his mind while he is still in that stage of his motoring education.

" Road Sense " is a very real thing, and it is a subject that can be self-taught. A person who has acquired road sense not only follows the instructions of the Highway Code *instinctively*, but develops a sort of second sight which enables him to anticipate things about to happen, and to prepare himself accordingly. Perhaps I should amend that and say " are likely to be about to happen," for, although he foresees, and prepares for, eventualities, they may not always actually come to pass.

For instance, there may be a group of children on the pavement ahead. They may be quite placid, and apparently likely to remain so. But, the driver with a fully developed road sense will find himself automatically preparing to make an emergency stop, and noting in his rear-view mirror that no vehicle is immediately behind him. If there were, he would give its driver a cautionary signal that he intended to slow down. The good driver does, indeed, pay a great amount of attention to his rear-view mirror, although he does it in such a way that it does not take his attention off the road ahead for more than the metaphorical flicker of an eyelid. He keeps himself continuously posted as to following traffic, especially in towns where he may need to move from one traffic lane to another.

On the open road, he will keep a wary eye cocked for side

turnings, and, if there are no hedges, he will glance to right and left along the intersecting road to gain an impression of whether a cyclist, a cart, or, perhaps, cattle, are to be expected. The last-named call for special attention in many parts of the country, for a cow may appear with considerable suddenness from a field path or farm lane, but the driver who has road sense will have noticed signs of their habitual presence from marks on the road or from traces in the neighbourhood.

In the same way, in mountainous districts like Wales and Scotland, sheep may be expected to materialise on the road with startling abruptness ; they will, however, be less of a shock to the driver with road sense, because he will have anticipated their presence and will always suspect that, if they are going to get in his way, they will do so at the most unexpected spot. He will, instinctively and pessimistically, assume that somebody or something will always be doing some fool thing round the corner.

When rounding a bend on a country road, he will anticipate that there will be two or three pedestrians spread out across the road and a cyclist or another car coming in the opposite direction. He will, therefore, blow his horn to signify his presence, but will not rely on this clearing his path ; he will have his car under such control that he can stop with certainty within range of his vision. But he will blow his horn to show that he is there, and in the hope that, if there should be another car coming, its driver will likewise warn of *his* presence.

As regards the use of the horn, the driver with road sense, while he does not blow it unnecessarily, or, shall I say, at places where the onus rests on him to be specially prudent, will not fail to use it as a means of signifying his presence on the road at points where that knowledge would be useful to other drivers. For example, on a narrow, twisty road, it is wise for two drivers to announce where they are when concealed one from the other. At a cross-roads where two main or semi-main roads meet, each driver should slow down to a pace from which he can bring his car to a stop, and not rely on the horn to clear his way.

It might here, perhaps, be mentioned that the rule of the road in Great Britain does not recognise priority being given to traffic coming from the right or the left of another vehicle. In certain Continental countries, notably France, there is a very strict rule that a driver gives way to another driver coming up on his right. By virtue of this, a driver has to keep a sharp watch for traffic on one side of him only, and does not, as we do in the United Kingdom, have to move his head from one side to another in order to keep a two-way look-out. It is this rule which keeps traffic moving rapidly, yet with reasonable safety, in the roundabouts of Paris and other large French towns, while to a British driver there seems danger threatening from every side. Let him follow suit, when in Paris, and he will find the traffic problem much simplified.

To return to the horn, however, there are some drivers who say with pride that they never make use of the one on their own car, and such drivers number among their ranks some of the best and most accident-free. My own personal opinion, however, is that judicious use of the horn is both necessary and desirable ; it should not be done as a command to other people to get off the road, but as a warning that one's car is approaching. It should be borne in mind that, in the event of an accident, one of the first questions a driver will be asked is : " Did you blow your horn ? " Remember that the law demands an audible warning of approach shall be given, and that, if only *one* accident can be prevented by such warning, the horn has proved its worth.

A driver who has taught himself road sense will be very particular as to where he leaves his car. If, for instance, he wishes to stop by the roadside, he will consider very carefully before coming to a standstill. If there should happen

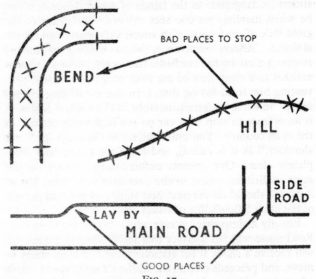

FIG. 17

The crosses denote places where a good driver will never stop his car. He will find a lay-by or a side road where his vehicle will not impede traffic flow.

to be a side road down which he could turn off the main highway, and so leave the latter clear, he will make use of it. Or, if there should be a verge on to which he could pull, he will do so. If, however, he must stop at the roadside, he will seek a stretch of road where his car will not impair the view of an oncoming driver. He would never park on a bend, or at the crest of a hill—or, worse still, just over the crest.

It is literally astonishing how many drivers lack road sense in this connection. A car when stationary can be almost as dangerous in the hands of a bad driver as it can be when moving, yet one sees evidence every day of the gross lack of road sense with which very many drivers are afflicted. Always remember, when parking or merely stopping a car by the roadside, that every passing driver is entitled to a clear view of the road and, if your car is preventing him from having that, then you are lacking in road sense. In some countries, notably in the United States, it is an offence to stop your car on the highway, even out in the open country. You must pull on to the verge (or " soft shoulder," as it is called), and leave the traffic lane completely clear. One cannot, unfortunately, always do the same in Britain, owing to the prevalence of kerbs, but at least one should do the next best thing, which is to get out of the other fellow's line of vision.

Equally as important is care when re-starting from rest. Road sense will tell a driver that traffic coming up behind will receive a shock if his stationary car suddenly starts to move, and proceeds on into the traffic stream ; that a driver whose attention may be momentarily off the road may quite conceivably run into his back before he gathers speed. Yet it is common to see cars pull off a parking place and proceed straight on the road, with a " take care of yourself " attitude. No good driver does such a thing ; he makes a careful survey of oncoming traffic in both directions before he sets his car in motion, and, if there is a vehicle coming which he can see he will clear easily, he will still give a signal, if only as a courtesy.

Now, signalling can be overdone. One sees a great deal
of unnecessary hand- and trafficator-waggling, and it is apt
to be a source of irritation to other drivers. Usually it
betokens that the person who is doing the signalling is
inexperienced—perhaps even doing his driving test. Do
not think that I am advocating against signalling ; I am
merely pointing out that signals, when given, should be
made clearly to inform other road users of an intention on
the part of a driver which it is necessary to reveal. It is the
ambiguous, unnecessary and obscure hand-waving that I
am decrying.

The Highway Code lays down and illustrates four signals
by which drivers of motor cars are to indicate their own
intentions, and points out that these signals are for the
purpose of giving information *and not instructions* to other
road users. The four signals are :—

1. " I am going to slow down or stop."
2. " I am going to turn to my right."
3. " I am ready to be overtaken."
4. " I am going to turn to my left."

These are the only four recognised signals, and, if made
properly, each is clear and distinctive. But how frequently
does one see obscure, ambiguous and unofficial signals
given ? Remember the *Punch* cartoon where a lady driver
is saying to a policeman, after an accident : " But I clearly
gave the signal that I had changed my mind ! "

The mechanical traffic indicator can perform only two
of the four signals, the turn to the right and the turn to the
left. Even in the case of the latter, it is not always wise to
rely on the indicator arm conveying the message to traffic
which is following at a fairly close range, since a driver who
is on your tail, and possibly intending to overtake, may not

be in a position to see the indicator arm on the far side of the car. In such cases, the good driver will give one of those instantaneous glances into his rear-view mirror and, if he sees that there is another vehicle close behind, he will give a hand signal as well as switch up his left-hand trafficator.

A driver with road sense will likewise use discretion as to how far he relies on his mechanical indicator to give clear and sufficient warning of his intentions. For instance, on a main road where there is fast traffic, a following driver may not be close enough to see that the indicator arm is out until it is too late to dive over to the left-hand side of the road in order to pass on the nearside while the driver who is signalling is waiting for an opportunity to turn to the right. There is also the matter of lighting conditions to be considered : I once had an unpleasant moment when, about to overtake another car on a fast stretch of arterial road, I suddenly realised that its indicator arm was out and that the driver was actually on the point of turning across the road on to a parking place. But what the good lady in charge of the car had not realised was that (a) there was no light showing inside her trafficator arm, and (b) the sun was dead ahead, fairly low in the sky, and the trafficator was almost blotted out by glare.

In such a case, a driver with well-developed road sense would have appreciated that someone was coming up behind, at a rapid pace, and needed a more clearly visible signal than even a properly-working trafficator could give, and would therefore have extended an arm to supplement the indicator.

Every car owner should, from time to time, make a check on the trafficators fitted to his vehicle, not only to see that they really are working but also to make certain that the light inside the arm is functioning. This last is highly important, because, without the glow inside the transparent red casing, a trafficator is not a very clearly visible signal.

I remember once having another narrow squeak when a car, restarting at traffic lights, suddenly pulled right across my bows and did, in fact, scrape my wing. I stopped the driver, after a chase, and asked him why he had not signalled his intention of turning. He replied that he had put out his trafficator, and, when I requested him to repeat the process, as I had certainly not seen the arm, he discovered that the arm was stuck in its recess, although the light inside it could be seen glowing when one stood by the side of the car.

The keynote of the Highway Code is " Consideration for others, as well as for yourself." If you let this sink in, you will always put yourself in the place of the other fellow, and ask yourself " Should I know what I am about to do ? " " Am I giving as much room as I can ? " " Is my car blocking his view ? " These are the things we all hope that the other driver will do for *us*, to the end that traffic may flow freely and with the maximum of safety.

And just one more point about signalling ; an exhortation to do it in good time. If you are going to turn, to stop or to slow down, let those who are following have adequate notice of your intentions. Bear in mind that the other man may possibly, at the instant you give your signal, have his attention momentarily occupied with some other detail and, therefore, if you give your signal at the very last instant, when you are on the point of carrying it into effect, he may not receive it until a fraction too late.

In traffic, if you are going to turn right immediately after a light signal, at which you have to stop, give an indication of your intention before you actually come to rest. The man behind may be going straight on, and, if you have not let him know beforehand, he may get shut in behind you if you are held up by oncoming traffic. You may thus cause delay to a whole string of vehicles, which could have been avoided with a little forethought.

The signs erected at the roadside for the warning and guidance of road users deserve, I think, rather more attention than is paid to them in the Highway Code. As regards speed, the signs illustrated in the Code are the 30 m.p.h. restriction and the cancellation thereof. Now, although, theoretically, there is no speed limit except in a restricted area, there are many places where the driver with good road sense will reduce speed to far below even the 30 m.p.h. prescribed for built-up areas. There was, in former days, a sign consisting merely of a red triangle, which indicated danger of one sort or another, and was a generalised recommendation to proceed with caution.

It is perhaps true that these triangles were erected in too great a profusion, and that they were put up at many points where the advice they gave was not entirely necessary. The fact remains, however, that the old, simple triangle has been done away with, and its place taken, but only at certain specified points, by cautionary signs which are amplified by an indication of the danger of which they foretell. These signs are surmounted by a triangle, point uppermost, and give warning of cross-roads, bends, narrow sections, level crossings, roundabouts, steep hills, road junctions and so forth. They are, of course, extremely useful, but there are, nevertheless, many dangerous points, especially on country roads, where the old, simple triangle was a helpful and timely warning. In its absence, a driver should always exercise great care when approaching a point in the road where a clear view is not obtainable, and should keep his speed in check so that he will be able to pull up within the range of vision. Such danger points are many and various ; they may even be caused by seasonal occurrences like a thick growth of hedge or the foliage of a tree. But the point I wish to make is that a good driver is always suspicious of lurking danger wherever his eye cannot penetrate. He always endeavours not to be taken by surprise and regulates his speed so that, as far as is humanly possible, he will never be caught with insufficient room in which to bring his car to a standstill.

One sign to which no reference is made in the Highway Code, yet one for which a driver should always be on the look-out, and obey implicitly, is the " No Entry " sign. This is used to denote that traffic is to pass in only one direction along a road or street, and consists either of a red disc with a white bar on which is lettered " No Entry," or a rectangular plaque, also in red, carrying the same wording. In the case of the latter, a red disc should surmount the plaque, but I am sorry to say that there has been a certain amount of laxity on the part of the highway authorities in Great Britain in complying with prescribed forms for road signs. None the less, the words "No Entry" are highly important to the motorist, for, if he fails to comply with the authorised direction of traffic flow, he may not only cause grave embarrassment to other drivers, but may be responsible for a collision at a corner where traffic, quite properly entering the one-way street on the offside of the road, may find his car already there and proceeding in the opposite direction.

I am often, quite frankly, amazed at the inattention of drivers to " No Entry " signs. Although, admittedly, the old rectangular type of sign is sometimes none too legible, while highway authorities frequently position the signs so

British mandatory signs.

British direction signs.

Recommended New Type

Existing Type

 RED BLUE

British prohibitory signs.

Prohibition of Traffic

No Entry

Customs House

No Parking

Obligatory Direction

No Waiting

Cross Roads

Dangerous Bend

Danger Ahead

Gully in Road

Gated Level Crossing

Ungated Level Crossing

International signs, used on the Continent.

British informative signs, which differ in some respects from the international code.

that they cannot readily be seen, there are, nevertheless, a considerable number of drivers who just fail to see them through, it appears, sheer inattention. I cannot stress too strongly that the injunction " No Entry " really does mean what it says, and that it should be considered a serious lapse to run past one without noticing it. At the same time, I would ask that those who are responsible for siting and erecting such signs should use every care to ensure that they are placed as prominently as ever possible.

The " Halt " sign is another which should be obeyed in the letter and the spirit. These signs are placed on secondary roads a short distance before their junction with a major road. The " Halt " sign is easily recognisable because the plaque beneath the triangle is swelled out horizontally and is not merely rectangular, like other warning signs. When encountering a " Halt " sign, the driver should proceed until he arrives at the junction with the major road, where a white line will be painted across the road. The car must be brought to a stop without crossing this line, and the driver must look both ways along the major road, and satisfy himself that there is no traffic coming from either direction along it which will be inconvenienced if he proceeds. Even should there be no traffic on the major road, there is an obligation on the driver emerging from the secondary road to bring his vehicle to a dead stop, and to fail to do so is an offence in the eyes of the law.

In the case of the sign which reads " Slow—major road ahead " the driver should slacken speed as he reaches the junction of the secondary and the major roads, and be prepared to stop if traffic conditions on the latter warrant his doing so. I might here mention that the triangles surmounting both the " Halt " and the " Slow " signs are inverted, so that the point is downwards. This is to distinguish these two " mandatory " signs from the ordinary " informative " signs such as " cross-roads," " bends," " narrow sections," and the others to which I referred previously.

One of the greatest difficulties with which a driver has to contend concerns the pedestrian crossing the road. In every town, and at numerous places in the country, there are pedestrian crossings which are officially designated as such, and are indicated by studs laid in the road surface, and often by " beacons " on the footpath. The regulations governing motorists at these crossings are that a pedestrian shall be given free passage, and that the motorist shall approach the crossing at a speed which will enable him to stop before reaching the crossing, *unless he can see that there is no pedestrian on the crossing*. I have emphasised those last words, because the chief problem which faces a driver is that pedestrians so often step off the pavement on to the crossing as the motorist approaches ; i.e., the pedestrian is not actually on the crossing until the last moment. Alternatively, the pedestrian may step on to the crossing, and then stop, or he may decide that he had better not risk it, and step back after having started to cross.*

As a driver gains experience, he acquires a technique which deals satisfactorily with the majority of normal cases. First, he approaches a pedestrian crossing with extreme caution, and glances to both sides of the road to ascertain whether any person is likely to make an unexpected step off the pavement. If the crossing is quite clear, and yet he senses that some intending crosser may make a dash for it, he gives a gentle toot with his horn to indicate his approach.

* At the time this book goes to press, revised regulations governing pedestrian crossings are under consideration.

If a pedestrian makes it obvious that he intends to cross in front of the car, the driver will give way, provided the available distance is reasonable and the road surface is not in a condition which might make it dangerous to apply the brakes forcibly. Should such be the case, it would be safer to give the pedestrian an emergency blast on the horn and hope that he will realise the driver's difficulty. One thing that a driver should appreciate, if he pulls up at a pedestrian crossing, is that other drivers coming up behind may not immediately understand why he has stopped, and that a pedestrian may be hidden from their view by his vehicle. It is usual to give the signal " I am going to slow down or stop " as a warning in such circumstances.

It is not the rule or custom in Great Britain to give priority to traffic on one's right or left, as I have pointed out. The only principle laid down by the Highway Code is that traffic on the major of two roads has priority. Where, for example, a secondary road joins or crosses a main road, even though there should be no " Halt " or " Slow " sign, a driver on the lesser road would give way. While this rule is fairly simple to apply in the case of roads that are either main or secondary, there are large numbers of crossings or junctions on secondary roads, more or less equal in importance. In the event of encountering another vehicle on roads such as these, a tacit agreement has to be arrived at with the other driver as to who shall take precedence. The thing to avoid is that both take precedence together !

A good driver, while not being too forceful or aggressive in encounters with other drivers, will nevertheless act with determination after giving clear and definite signals as to his intentions. He will maintain a clear-cut and decisive course while under way, and will not wander from one traffic lane to another unnecessarily. He will, by the

proper use of his rear-view mirror, keep himself continually posted as to other vehicles that may be coming up
behind, and, if they seem intent on proceeding at a faster
pace than he does, he will choose a suitable stretch of road
and then, pulling towards the nearside edge of the road,
will give the signal " I am ready to be overtaken." He
himself will overtake only when he can see an adequate
distance ahead, and, if the road is not wide enough to give
much spare clearance, he will acquaint the other driver
that he is overtaking by the medium of his horn.

When stopping by the roadside, or parking, he will
draw his car clear of the traffic lane, or, if that is not possible,
will choose a section of road where other drivers will not
find their vision blocked by his vehicle. He will always try
to avoid stopping on the " wrong " side of the road (i.e.,
with the car facing oncoming traffic), and he most certainly
will not do so at night. After dark, whenever he stops, he
will switch off his headlamps, and will go round to the
back of his car to assure himself that his rear light is in
proper working order. He will never allow things to dangle
on his windscreen or at his rear window. If he has owned the
same car for a long time, you will probably find it is free
from dents, scratches and other evidence of having fallen
foul of other road users. The man with a crumpled car is
hardly likely to be *always* the victim of other people's
carelessness.

If I may go on to amplify the ethics of night driving, I
would add that the considerate motorist will check up on
his headlamps' beam from time to time, and make sure that
he is not inadvertently dazzling other road users because
of some perhaps unsuspected defect. When the headlamps
are mounted in such a way that they can be swivelled—
even if unintentionally—when pushing the car inside a

garage, it is easy for them to direct their rays to one side, possibly only slightly, but still sufficiently for an odd beam to be diverted towards the eye of a passing driver. It is quite simple to eradicate this annoyance, and most good garages now have testing apparatus by means of which a complete check up on the setting and focusing of headlamps can be carried out efficiently and rapidly.

The Highway Code calls on motorists not to use their headlamps unnecessarily, especially in lighted areas, and to dip them when meeting other vehicles unless there are exceptional circumstances which make it unsafe to do so. It also tells drivers to switch off or dip their headlights when following close behind another vehicle which they do not intend to overtake. I would myself go further, and say that, even when you do intend to overtake, the headlamps should be kept dipped until the overtaking has actually been done. Also, the driver who has been overtaken ought then to dip ; unfortunately, there is too often the tendency for the over-taken one to say to himself " Oh, so you think you can drive faster than me, do you—well, I'll dazzle you from behind if I can."

One point which I think the Highway Code might well have mentioned more prominently is that it is an offence when you stop your car (except in traffic conditions) after dark to leave your headlamps alight. How often does one come across cars which are halted, or perhaps parked, at the roadside with one or both headlamps shining full into oncoming drivers' eyes ? For some reason, a stationary vehicle with its headlamps alight seems to be more objectionable—dangerous, perhaps, is the word—than an oncoming one. I cannot too strongly emphasise that the law requires that headlamps must be turned off when a car is brought to rest after dark.

c

Dazzle on roads which are as congested as those of this country are becoming is one of the most worrying things that a night driver has to face, and anything that can be done to improve the position is absolutely necessary in the general interest. The system of dipping headlamps which has been developed by British firms is probably the best of any in general use throughout the world. I have driven in the U.S.A. and throughout Europe, and I find less difficulty in meeting British cars with dip-and-switch mechanism than with cars of other nationalities which have dimmers. The latter are merely bulbs of smaller power than the normal headlamps, but the beam usually remains focused straight ahead, whereas in our case it is directed downwards.

In France the law obliges motorists to use headlamps with a yellow tint, either by the employment of a coloured bulb or a front glass. While this is perhaps useful when driving in fog, since it seems that the beam can pierce through it farther without causing a shroud of reflected light, it is in my opinion doubtful whether, in ordinary conditions, there is any less dazzle because the light is yellow.

Some Queries to Ask Yourself at this Point

1.—What are the five principal controls of a car and their respective uses ?

2.—Do the front wheels remain parallel at all times, and, if not, why not ?

3.—What is the reason for the clutch, and how does it function ?

4.—How is it possible for brakes to catch fire ?

5.—What effect does the accelerator have on the throttle ?

6.—Why should a car require several different gear ratios, and what is understood by the term " changing down " ?

7.—What is meant by " double-declutching," and how has the necessity for this been eliminated from modern cars ?

8.—When is it necessary to use the choke, and for how long ?

9.—A tell-tale light shows when the ignition has been switched on. Why does it go out, and when ?

10.—What are the operations, in their proper sequence, for starting a car into motion ?

11.—When should a driver change gear ?

12.—What is the right technique for driving a car round a bend ?

13.—What traffic receives priority on British roads ?

14.—Give a few examples of points at which a driver should NOT park his car.

15.—What are the four " official " signals for car drivers to indicate their intentions to other traffic ?

16.—How far should a driver rely on his mechanical trafficators ?

17.—Which road signs have the points of the surmounting triangle inverted ?

18.—How should a driver proceed in regard to pedestrian crossings ?

19.—What is the code of behaviour in respect of head-lamps ?

20.—How should a battery be maintained in good condition ?

PART II

THE "WORKS"

IN order to be able to handle a car properly, and to get the best out of it, a certain amount of knowledge of the internal workings of a motor engine and the other component parts of the vehicle is very desirable. I do not, by this, mean that every driver should be a mechanic, or, indeed, possess the skill necessary to dismantle and reassemble an engine, gearbox or any other major part. It is, however, most useful to be able to perform simple jobs, since there is no knowing when, for example, a speck of dust may choke the carburettor or an electric wire jump out of its socket and cause an ignition breakdown. Both these minor ailments, I might add, have occurred to me on cars that were in a practically new state. In each case, the trouble was rectified in a few moments, but it was necessary to know, when the engine stopped, where the defect had most probably occurred.

It is the ability to detect the cause—or perhaps I should say to forestall the cause—of breakdown that is valuable to a motorist. He acquires this ability by understanding what is going on inside each of the major components of his car, and by an appreciation of the functions of the ancillary parts, such as springs, brakes, steering gear and so forth. He can avert trouble and undue wear by a sympathetic realisation of what is happening to some working part which is hidden away from normal view, yet is in an exposed position so far as wet mud and dust thrown up from the road are concerned.

Let us, therefore, make a survey of the " works " of a motor-car, and, without going too deeply into technicalities, acquaint ourselves with the theory and, to a certain extent, the practice, of the component parts. In passing, I might mention that, if certain passages in my description of a car's controls in the earlier section of this book have seemed a trifle involved for a learner, it may help if the following descriptions are read through and then further reference made to the earlier section in the light of the knowledge now gained. Let us start with the main component of a car—the engine.

Engine

Whoever it was that first discovered explosive properties when certain substances were mixed was the real " father " of the internal combustion engine. A motor of the kind fitted to a car is, by the way, always termed internal combustion, or " i.c.," because the combustion which produces the power takes place inside it. The steam engine, by contrast, is supplied with its raw material from outside, the combustion which raises the temperature to produce the steam occurring externally. In both cases—and in the case of every form of power producer that has ever been invented—it is heat that causes power to be developed, and every type of engine is merely a machine which transforms heat from fuel of one sort or another into movement. The amount of movement and the force that accompanies it are dependent on the amount of fuel consumed and the efficiency of the particular design of engine in which it is being consumed.

To revert for a moment to that " father " of the internal combustion engine, to whom I referred just now, he was probably the man who discovered gunpowder, likewise the fact that a heavy ball of lead could be tossed quite a long way by causing the explosion to take place inside a strong container, which developed into a gun. I believe that some sort of an internal combustion engine was made centuries ago, for raising water from a well, by utilising the principle of exploding a charge of gunpowder in a long barrel, with a rope attached to what could be termed the cannon ball.

At any rate, that is the principle on which a motor car engine works, and, if we go to a circus and see some fair lady blown from the mouth of a cannon, we may reflect that we are witnessing the process that goes on continuously inside the cylinders of our motor car. Admittedly, we do not use gunpowder to cause the explosion, but there is no reason why we should not, other than the unwieldiness of its nature. In point of fact, at one period in the very early days of motors, powdered coal was employed as the explosive agent. Before that, however, coal gas was used as the medium, and I have a woodcut in my possession showing a dogcart with a cylinder in which gas was exploded to drive a piston connected to the back axle of the vehicle by a connecting rod and crank. The driver and his lady passenger are shown sitting on the gasbag, their weight forcing its contents through to the engine. Coal gas has, more recently, been pressed into service through lack of liquid fuel in wartime.

It was the discovery of liquid fuel that really gave the motor car a chance of success. Although I will not vouch for it being an historical fact, the story is that, when Carl Benz, the first man to build a practicable motor vehicle, was experimenting, his attention was drawn to the possibility of using vaporised petroleum spirit by an accident reported in his local paper. A woman, it seemed, had been washing her hair in benzine when an explosion occurred through the vapour coming into contact with a lighted candle. What happened to the unfortunate woman is not recorded, but Benz devised an apparatus for gasifying the spirit and conveying the gas to the cylinder of his engine.

We do not use, to-day, the same system of gasifying petroleum spirit—petrol, as we call it for short, the name having been coined by one of the firms producing it (Carless, Capel and Leonard) half-a-century ago—but the component that does it for us is still of prime importance. We call it the carburettor, and, if you look up the word " carburet " in a dictionary, you will find it means " to combine with carbon." Now, as we know, coal is a carbon ; petrol is a hydro-carbon, or liquid version of coal. Neither coal nor petrol is explosive *of itself*; it is, therefore, the duty of the carburettor to combine with the carbon something that produces such capability. What is it ? Why, air from the atmosphere. (The scientist, of course, would tell us that it is really only the oxygen in the air that is used for the purpose.)

The carburettor, therefore, is an apparatus for combining petrol from the car's tank with air from the atmosphere, mixing them in the right proportion and delivering the resultant gas to the engine. It has to perform all this to order, so to speak, the order coming from the driver of the car through the medium of his foot on the accelerator pedal. As he presses his foot down, the rods linking the accelerator pedal with the carburettor cause the throttle valve in the outlet pipe of the carburettor to open wider ; this pipe forms one with the induction pipe of the engine, and so, the harder the pressure on the accelerator, the greater the volume of gas passing through to the engine. Naturally, the more it gets, the stronger will be the explosions occurring inside the cylinders and therefore the faster the engine will run, or the harder it will pull.

The manner in which the carburettor transforms liquid petrol into a very good semblance of gas is to pass the

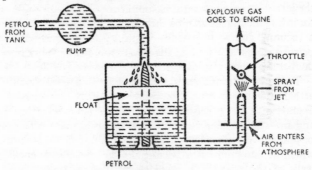

FIG. 18

A diagrammatic illustration of how petrol is transformed into a fine spray and mixed with air to form an explosive mixture.

petrol through a tiny hole under considerable pressure and, as it emerges in the form of a spray, to bring air in to mingle with it from a pipe communicating with the atmosphere. The petrol finds its way to the carburettor by being drawn along a pipe from the tank at the rear of the car through the agency of a special pump. This is usually situated on the side of the engine, below the carburettor, and is actuated either by electricity or by a plunger connecting with a moving part of the engine. The pump draws petrol from the tank, and then pushes it up to the carburettor, where it enters what is called the float chamber. As its level in this chamber rises, so a light metal float goes up also, and, having reached the pre-determined level, plugs a needle into the hole which allows the petrol to enter and so cuts off the supply until the level has fallen again.

Once in the float chamber the petrol finds itself being urged to pass through a passage into the jet chamber and, as we already know, through the tiny hole which constitutes the jet. The urge behind it is supplied by the engine itself, for inside the induction pipe there is something approaching a vacuum, and so it is really suction that is drawing the petrol through the jet and the air in from outside. Where does this suction originate ?

To provide the answer to that we must now examine the actual manner in which an internal combustion engine operates. It has a cylinder—several of them, probably— and in each cylinder a piston goes up and down. As the piston is a very close fit, and has springy " rings " round it which fit into grooves cut in its sides and press against the walls of the cylinder, it is practically impossible for any gas or air to leak past the piston. Accordingly, if we tried to pull the piston out of the cylinder with our hand, we

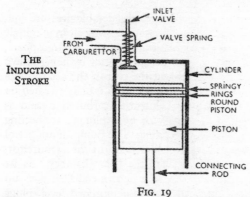

FIG. 19

How the inlet valve when open permits gas from the carburettor to enter the cylinder.

should only be able to get it a little way, because the vacuum we should create would be very strong, and become stronger the farther we pulled the piston down the cylinder.

If, however, we could open an aperture at the top end of the cylinder, we should transfer the suction to any pipe that might be connected with the aperture. If that pipe were the induction pipe that we were talking about just now, all the suction would be put upon the carburettor, and so the petrol and air would be drawn through it. That, indeed, is just the way in which the engine does get its charge of gas. But what is that aperture I mentioned ? And, if it allows gas to be sucked in, why does it not get blown out again when the piston goes back up the cylinder ?

The reason is that the aperture is controlled by a valve, the inlet valve. It is spring-loaded, and only stays open so long as something pushes it up and holds it there. Once left to its own devices, the spring brings the valve back on to its seat and it stays shut, so that communication

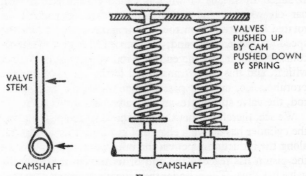

FIG. 20

A diagrammatic illustration of the method whereby the camshaft lifts the valves off their seat. A tappet is interposed between cam and valve stem in actual practice.

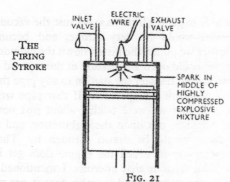

THE FIRING STROKE

INLET VALVE · ELECTRIC WIRE · EXHAUST VALVE

SPARK IN MIDDLE OF HIGHLY COMPRESSED EXPLOSIVE MIXTURE

FIG. 21

An electric spark occurs in the midst of highly compressed explosive mixture and fires it.

between the cylinder and the carburettor, via the induction pipe, is broken. To permit gas to be drawn into the engine, therefore, the valve must be opened at the commencement of the piston's stroke, and closed at the end of it. This is arranged by means of what is called a camshaft, a steel bar on which certain protuberances are formed. It is rotated by a drive from the main engine shaft, at half the speed of the engine, and, as each of the protuberances comes round, it lifts the end of a rod which lies in contact with it, and this lift is transmitted to the valve. When the protuberance, or cam, passes from under the end of the rod, the valve spring presses the valve back on its seat.

We see, therefore, that the movement of the piston along the cylinder has drawn a charge of gas from the carburettor along the induction pipe, via the inlet valve and that, when the piston has reached the end of its travel, or stroke, the valve has shut. The cylinder thus contains a filling of petrol-and-air vapour. When the piston moves back up its path, as it does by reason of the movement transmitted to it from the main shaft of the engine through the connecting rod, this gas is compressed. When the piston reaches the top of its stroke, it is very highly compressed indeed. And now, if we put a spark in that extremely explosive mixture, something pretty fierce is going to happen.

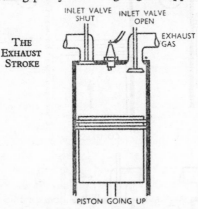

THE
EXHAUST
STROKE

FIG. 22

The exhaust valve opens and allows the piston to clear the remains of the burnt charge to be expelled from the cylinder, ready for the new charge to be inhaled.

What does happen is that the piston is driven hard down the cylinder, transmitting the force behind it to the engine main shaft, just as that same crankshaft supplied it with the energy to compress the gas on its previous movement along the cylinder. But what about when the piston reaches the end of this combustion stroke—how does it get rid of its fill of burnt gas ?

This is where a second valve—the exhaust valve—comes into play. Designed and operated in similar fashion to the inlet valve, it opens when the piston is nearly at the end of

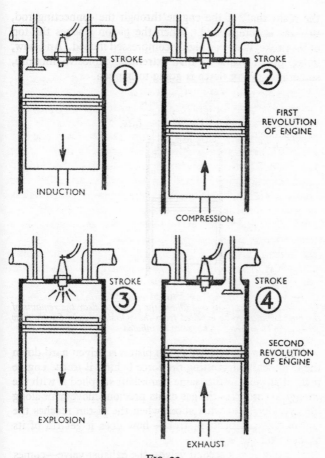

STROKE ①

FIRST REVOLUTION OF ENGINE

INDUCTION

STROKE ②

COMPRESSION

STROKE ③

SECOND REVOLUTION OF ENGINE

EXPLOSION

STROKE ④

EXHAUST

FIG. 23
A diagrammatic illustration of the four strokes (two revolutions of the engine) which constitute the " Otto cycle."

its power stroke and, on the return journey, the piston sweeps the burnt gas before it out through an exhaust aperture uncovered by this second valve, which communicates with a pipe that leads the unwanted products of combustion to the back of the car. Here they are discharged into the atmosphere.

We have therefore traced the complete cycle of operations of the motor engine, the four strokes, or " Otto cycle " as they are named after their inventor. Dr. Otto was one of a group of German gas-engine experts who did much in the last quarter of the nineteenth century to bring the internal combustion motor to fruition. Until he devised the four separate strokes, completed in two revolutions of the engine, of which the compression stroke was all-important, this type of engine was never very successful. Although power is apparently wasted in two extra, non-productive strokes, the benefit resulting from compressing the mixture before firing it is so immense that Otto's cycle of operations soon carried all before it.

At the time of writing there is only one car made for sale in the ordinary way that has a motor functioning on any other principle. This has an alternative, known as the two-stroke, and many motor cycles have engines of this type. The two-stroke-engined car is the German-built D.K.W. It may be as well, therefore, to deal briefly with this method of operation.

With a two-stroke, each outward movement of the piston is an induction stroke and power stroke combined, and each inward movement a compression-cum-exhaust stroke. For the first portion of the outward stroke the combustion of the gas is taking place, and, at the same time, compression of a new charge of gas is taking place in the crank-chamber. At the latter part of its outward stroke,

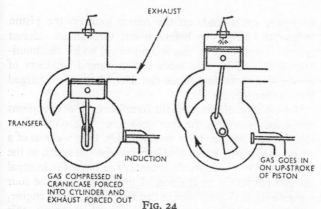

FIG. 24

A two-stroke engine completes its cycle of operations in one revolution of the engine. The gas is inhaled into the crankcase and then forced through a transfer port at the lower end of the piston's travel. The incoming charge expels the burnt gas. Note that the purpose of an inlet valve is usually served by the piston itself.

the piston uncovers what are known as "transfer ports," cut in the walls of the cylinder and communicating with the crank-chamber. Immediately these are cleared by the top of the piston, the compressed charge rushes into the cylinder from the crank-chamber, and, at the same time, the burnt gas is expelled through ports on the other side of the cylinder walls. The incoming charge, in fact, helps to clear the burnt gas out. As the piston moves inward, it closes both sets of ports, and the new charge is then compressed, being fired when the piston reaches the top of its stroke, and the cycle begins over again. The two-stroke engine is not popular for cars, since it is not so efficient in its running as the four-stroke, and cannot be made to run with any degree of regularity at low speeds when idling. A two-stroke engine fitted to a van (the Trojan) has a four-cylinder engine, of which two cylinders are for charging the other two, which do the work.

While on the subject of internal combustion engine principles, it might be as well to touch on two other types which are not, at the present time, in use for cars. One of these is the Diesel, while the other is the gas turbine. The former is used extensively for commercial vehicles, buses and coaches, but has never been successfully developed, so far, in small sizes suitable for private cars. The gas turbine is in the experimental stage where cars are concerned, although it has been demonstrated by the Rover Company that there are definite possibilities in this field.

The principle of the Diesel engine is that air, when compressed to a sufficiently high degree, generates of itself enough heat to ignite fuel oil (a product of the refining of petroleum which is a little less volatile than paraffin).

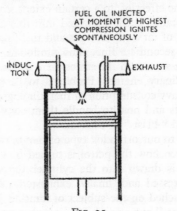

FIG. 25

A Diesel engine does not have an ignition system, as the fuel oil is caused to ignite when it is forced into the combustion chamber at the point of highest compression.

While the cycle of operations is the same as the Otto cycle, in the case of a four-stroke Diesel engine, there is no carburettor, and nothing but air is drawn in on the induction stroke. This is very highly compressed and, at the moment of greatest compression, a tiny quantity of fuel oil is injected into the cylinder head. It ignites instantaneously, and the resultant power and exhaust strokes are the same as in the case of the petrol engine. A Diesel engine has to be built much more strongly than its petrol-consuming counterpart, and accordingly weighs and costs considerably more. As it possesses little or no advantages for private cars it seems to have little future in this direction.

The gas turbine works on what is, after all, a very similar principle to the ordinary type of car engine, but pistons are replaced by rotating blades. Air is drawn in by a " blower " turbine revolving at a very high rate of speed, which has the effect of, to a certain extent, compressing it. Petrol or paraffin is then injected into this air, ignited to form a blast of intensely hot gas and this impinges on the blades of a second turbine, thus producing power. The burnt gas passes out to the atmosphere in the same way as with an ordinary engine. Problems to be overcome include the heavy consumption of fuel, the high speed of the rotating parts and how to handle them conveniently, and the noise and " blast " of the exhaust.

Reverting to our orthodox type of motor car engine, we have now seen how the petrol is turned into an explosive gas, how it is drawn into the cylinder through the inlet valve, compressed and, finally, exhausted. We have not, however, touched on the subject of igniting it, other than to say that we " put a spark into it." Let us consider the means whereby that spark arrives in the centre of the explosive mixture at the instant it is needed.

The ignition system of a car is, nowadays, a part of the complete electrical equipment of the vehicle, and not, as was once the case, a separately-generated current emanating from a magneto. On all cars of modern make, by which I

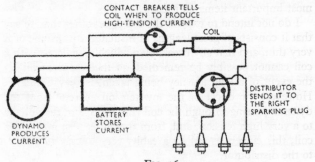

FIG. 26
A diagrammatic illustration of an electrical ignition system showing the function of all the component parts.

mean of 1930 and onwards, there is one single generator of electricity, a dynamo driven from the engine, which provides current for all the services requiring it. One of these is the ignition, and the manner in which this operates I will now describe.

The spark which ignites the explosive mixture is made to occur at the points of a sparking plug, which is screwed into the cylinder head. In its working position, the points are right in the midst of the gas when fully compressed; they have a gap of about twenty thousandths of an inch between them, and it is across this gap that the electric spark jumps. Now, current of the intensity that will jump such a gap, under high compression, has to have a high tension; in other words, it has to be at a pressure of several thousand volts, as compared with the twelve or six volts that suffice for the lights and other services of the car. To transform current from the six or twelve volts at which it is generated by the dynamo to two or three thousand volts, it has to pass through a coil, a piece of equipment which is one of the most important items on the car.

I do not intend to explain the coil here, other than to say that it consists of great lengths of insulated wire, some of it very thin, and that any breakdown which may occur with a coil cannot possibly be remedied, so that a spare coil, in the event of a long journey being taken, is very desirable. However, the effect of the low-tension current from the dynamo passing through the coil is to transform the voltage to a very high tension, and, from the outlet terminal of the coil, this current is led by a cable, very thickly insulated, to the distributor.

The action of the distributor is to send the high-tension current to the sparking plug of each cylinder in turn. It does this through the medium of a rotating contact arm (the rotor arm), and, as the piston in each cylinder is reaching the top of its compression stroke, the arm is making contact with the stud from which a cable runs to the required cylinder. The high-tension ignition current is thereby distributed to the right sparking plug at exactly the right instant to cause the spark to appear in the midst of the highly compressed explosive gas, with results that we have seen.

I mentioned that every engine develops its power by taking heat from its fuel and turning it into movement. In the case of the motor, the amount of heat abstracted from the fuel would be far too great to allow of the engine running satisfactorily for long unless it were for two factors —the cooling and the lubrication systems. In effect, they are both cooling systems, for the lubricating oil acts as an internal coolant, being thrown into places like the inside of the piston and abstracting heat after the manner of a cool shower falling on a hot body and then returning to the reservoir. It has to be appreciated that the heat of the continual explosions inside the cylinder is sufficient to raise the metal to red heat, as those who have travelled by aeroplane after dark will know.

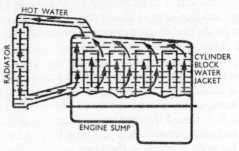

FIG. 27

Thermo-syphon cooling relies for its circulation upon the fact that hot water rises and cold falls. The change of direction occurs inside the radiator by reason of the current of cool air passing through it as the car moves forward.

The majority of cars have a system of water-cooling for their engines, although air blown by fans through ducts on to the cylinders is sometimes employed instead, on small cars. A water-cooled engine has the water jackets cast around the cylinder block, and the circulation through them is either by pump or by thermo-syphon. The latter principle makes use of the fact that hot water will always rise, and cool water fall. Thus, water entering at the lowest part of the system will rise as it becomes warmer, and will pass out of the jacket at its highest point, if connected to a closed circulation system.

Always, somewhere in the water circulation system, there is a radiator, which takes the hot water and passes it through tubes or gills that provide as great an area of cooling surface as is practicable. In this radiator the water, as it loses its heat, falls to the bottom and thence passes along a pipe to enter the cylinder block once more at the lowest point. A fan is usually fitted to assist the radiator in dissipating the water's heat, and it is incumbent on the driver to ensure that the radiator is kept always topped up—specially important in the case of thermo-syphon circulation.

The lubrication system of most cars embodies an oil pump, which is located in the very bottom of the sump, or crank-chamber, and is driven from the engine. The sump holds a considerable quantity of oil—a gallon or more is quite usual—and this is circulated continuously by the pump. It is forced through passages drilled in the crankshaft, and feeds out at each of the main bearings and also at the " big-ends," which is the bearing where the big end of the connecting rods is attached to the crankshaft. (The little end of the connecting rod, in the piston, is known as the " gudgeon pin " bearing.)

Oil is also forced to the camshaft bearings, and to the ends of the " tappet rods," which, as we have seen, are caused by the rotating of the camshaft to rise at the proper time and open the inlet and exhaust valves. If the valves are of what is known as the overhead type, meaning that they are located in the cylinder head, and not in the lower portion, or cylinder itself, the rocker shaft over the head of the engine will also receive a forced feed of oil. The cylinder walls are lubricated by oil which sprays and splashes about inside the engine while it is running, and the little ends of the connecting rods get theirs from the same source.

Proper and efficient lubrication plays a most important

part in the good running and long life of any engine. To starve it of ample supplies of the best quality oil that can be bought is poor economy, and damage thus caused can never be undone. It is excellent policy to drain the sump of oil, and throw the old oil away, every 1,000 miles. At the same time, do not overfill the sump, as the excess may find its way to places where it is not desirable. Adhere always to the manufacturer of the car's recommendations.

Let us now recapitulate what we have so far learned about the working of the car engine. In the first place, it is called an internal combustion engine because the " fire " takes place inside the cylinder. The charge which combusts is a mixture of gasified petrol and air ; the petrol is drawn from the tank by a pump, which is either electrically operated or receives its impulses from a mechanical attachment to the moving parts of the engine. This pump " pushes " the petrol into the carburettor, where it enters first the float chamber, so called because there is a float which rises with the level of the petrol and, at the proper height, cuts off any more supply until what is already there has been used. If this were not done, the carburettor would be continually " flooding " because petrol was coming in faster than it was being used up. (This sometimes happens inadvertently when a speck of dust or grit lodges in the seating of the needle valve which the float actuates when it rises.)

The carburettor is a piece of apparatus that transforms the liquid petrol into a finely divided spray by passing it through a tiny hole, called the jet. As it issues from the jet, it is made to mix with a column of air which is being drawn in from the atmosphere. The proper proportion for normal combustion of petrol to air is as one is to (about) fourteen ; when there is more petrol, the mixture is said to be " rich." A rich mixture is required for starting-up purposes, and this is effected by the driver pulling out a "choke" control on the facia board, which shuts down the area of the inlet through which air passes from the atmosphere into the carburettor. It is highly important that the choke be put out of action as soon as ever the engine will fire evenly without a rich mixture. (We will enter into the reason for this a little later on.)

The gaseous mixture, when it leaves the carburettor, is highly explosive. It passes along a pipe, known as the induction pipe, and enters the engine. It is caused to do this by suction arising from a piston which is travelling down a cylinder; the engine may have two, four, six or more cylinders—each, of course, with its own piston—and the gas goes into every cylinder in turn because, as any particular piston starts its suction, or induction, stroke, an inlet valve is made to open. This valve is normally held on its seat by a strong spring, but a camshaft driven by the mainshaft of the engine, at half its speed, forces a tappet rod upwards and this, acting through a rocker arm, raises the valve from its seat for the exact period during which the piston is travelling along the cylinder on its induction stroke.

When the piston reaches the end of its travel, the connecting rod by which it is attached to the mainshaft of the engine sends it back up the cylinder again, this time on the compression stroke. The explosive gas is now packed tighter and tighter because the cylinder is a completely closed chamber. When the piston reaches the top of this stroke, therefore, the gas is compressed to an extremely high degree. (Just what the degree is varies with different types of engine; the average touring car may have an engine with a compression ratio of seven to one, while a racing car may have one with a ratio of twelve to one. The ratio means the difference in volume between the full capacity of the cylinder, or the " volume swept " by the piston on any one of its strokes, and the volume into which the gas is compressed at the top of the piston's stroke.)

At the point where the gas is almost fully compressed, the sparking plug is caused to produce an electric spark in the heart of the now highly-explosive charge. It does this because a current of very high voltage, or " tension," is passed to it from the distributor, which in turn has received it from the coil. The latter transforms the ordinary six or twelve volt, low tension, current which comes from the car's dynamo into a high voltage one by passing it through a long coil of thin wire, enabling it to attain sufficient intensity to jump the spark gap formed by the points of the sparking plug. You will have noted that I said it does this at the point where the gas is " almost " fully compressed. The spark is, in fact, advanced a little—made to occur before the piston reaches the top of the compression stroke, in other words—because the combustion, or explosion, of the gas is not absolutely instantaneous. The flame takes a minute fraction of time to spread through the tightly-packed mixture, and, by starting the combustion a trifle previously, the explosion has attained its fullest pressure when the piston reaches the end of its stroke—" top dead centre," it is called—and so imparts the maximum of force to it as it starts to go down on the working, or power development, stroke.

The amount of advance which is given to the ignition, that is, the distance prior to reaching top dead centre at which the spark is made to occur, depends on the type of engine and the nature of the fuel being used. An engine runs faster, and more economically, by being given advanced ignition, but a point can be reached where the explosion is being caused prematurely. The engine is then apt to "knock," or "pink," giving off a noise, when pulling under load, which is unpleasant and may be distressing to the driver and occupants of the car. It is as if a hammer were knocking on an anvil, and arises from detonation of the gas inside the cylinder ; it is known, also, as "pre-ignition." The remedy is either to retard the spark, i.e., setting it to occur a little later, or to use a better grade of petrol. If the latter is not available—as is the case in Britain at the time of writing—the ignition timing must be set back until the pinking disappears, a job quite easily done by a mechanic. Some car manufacturers provide for adjustment of the ignition timing by fitting a hand-operated control which revolves the distributor head slightly and produces the required effect ; on others, there is an automatic advance and retard mechanism operated by centrifugal force (i.e., advancing the ignition as the engine speed increases), or by a device actuated by engine suction in the induction pipe. The effect is to retard or advance as the engine requires.

An engine also "knocks" through an accumulation of carbon in the combustion chamber. This occurs when an engine has covered some considerable mileage, and is not to be confused with too early ignition timing. The pre-ignition in a dirty engine is caused by tiny particles of carbon, composed of burnt oil, becoming white hot and taking upon themselves, prematurely, the duty which is intended to be performed by the sparking plug. I will deal with this in the later section of this book, as it comes under the heading of maintenance.

Returning to our exposition of the working of an engine, we left the piston being forced down its stroke by the explosion, or combustion, of the compressed charge.

The power derived from this one stroke out of four is, of course, the reason why the engine drives the car, and, quite obviously, the amount of power which is developed is dependent on the volume of gas which was drawn into the cylinder on the induction stroke. The engine is not always running at its fullest power, and its " flexibility," or variation in power development, also its speed, are governed by the degree to which the driver presses on the accelerator pedal and consequently opens the throttle valve in the carburettor.

Running fast or slow, however, when the piston arrives at the end of the power stroke, the cylinder is more or less filled with burnt gas, which has expended its force, and now must be got rid of in order to make way for a new charge. Just before the piston comes to the bottom dead centre—again, to give a " lead " (for realise that all this is happening in a minute space of time)—the exhaust valve opens and remains open until the upcoming piston has swept all the gas out of the cylinder and into the exhaust pipe. The four-stroke, or Otto, cycle of operations has now been completed.

A few words may here be inserted concerning the exhaust system of a car. We have seen that it connects up with the outlet from the cylinder which is uncovered when the exhaust valve opens, and that it receives the " burnt " gas. " Burning " would probably be a truer word, since—especially when the engine is pulling hard, on full throttle—there is still a certain amount of flame present. I mentioned that those who have travelled in an aeroplane by night probably realise that parts of an internal combustion engine operate at red heat, and, while a water-cooled car engine may not normally run as hot as an air-cooled aero-engine, the fact remains that the burnt, or burning, gas is at a very high temperature when it leaves the cylinder and enters the exhaust system.

For this reason, the "manifold," which is bolted to the side of the cylinder and receives the gas as it leaves the exhaust port, is made of thick cast iron; it is the hottest

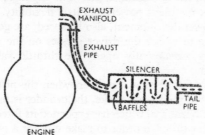

FIG. 28

A diagrammatic illustration of the path followed by the exhaust gases leaving the engine. They pass out of the tail pipe into the atmosphere.

part of the car, and, if you raise the bonnet during the course of a run, you must take care not to let your hand come into contact with the manifold. Sometimes the manifold is ribbed to assist cooling, but, in any case, the gas has lost a good deal of its sting when it leaves the manifold and enters the exhaust pipe proper. This conducts it to the exhaust box, or "silencer," which is usually located under the floor of the car, with a tail pipe to lead the gas to the extreme rear. The silencer consists of a long cylinder and is, in reality, an expansion chamber wherein the gas can lose its velocity and its remaining pressure before passing out into the atmosphere.

We all know that, whereas a motor cycle is often very noisy, the average car is comparatively quiet. The difference in their respective noises is entirely due to the fact that, on a car, the silencer can be made of sufficient capacity to allow the gas to expand and " normalise " itself before reaching the outer world, whereas the amount of space available on a motor cycle is restricted. If we disconnect the exhaust manifold from the cylinders, and run the engine, the exhaust noise will be as great as with a motor cycle ; in point of fact, the noise we hear is not, as some people imagine, the actual explosion taking place in the cylinder, but the impact of exhaust gas at high velocity on the atmosphere as it leaves the engine. The expansion chamber, or silencer, is generally equipped internally with baffle plates, which compel the gases to take a circuitous path and not allow them to pass straight through and out before having been adequately " toned down." A silencer is often believed to cause loss of power to an engine, but, provided its capacity is sufficient and it is not of inefficient design, or clogged internally with carbon deposit, the amount of power lost by reason of it is extremely little.

We noted, earlier, that the engine of most cars is cooled by a system of water jackets, which surround the cylinders and combustion chambers. They are cast in one piece with the cylinder block and head, and are not, therefore, apparent externally. About all that can be seen by looking at the outside of an engine are the water pipes leading into the cylinder jacket, low down, and emerging from the head. If, as is almost always the case, the cylinder head is detachable, there must be free connection between the water passages in the cylinder block and those in the head—yet, of course, there must also be a gas-tight joint between the two components which can be broken to permit of the head being detached. This joint must obviously also be water-tight and heat-resisting, and must have various shaped apertures in it to coincide with the water passages. It requires, in short, a highly complicated sort of " washer " to make it ; its technical name is " gasket," and it is compounded of copper and asbestos. Every car's cylinder-head gasket is of a different shape, and every time the head is taken off, for decarbonising or any other reason, a new gasket must be fitted.

The cooling water is circulated through the engine's jackets and then through the radiator. The majority of cars have a pump to effect this, a rotary vane-type of circulator not unlike the air purifiers which are fitted to windows, or an electric fan working in water. The pump is generally driven by a belt from a pulley fixed to the front end of the engine main shaft, and the pump spindle usually carries a fan on its forward extremity. The latter is to assist the cooling flow of air through the radiator, and, if a car has got to operate in very hot climates, there may be a two-speed gear to make the fan revolve faster than would be required elsewhere. On some small cars, the water circulation is of thermo-syphon type, which means that the natural rise of hot water and fall of cold water will cause flow from the radiator into cylinder jacket and from cylinder head into radiator. A mechanically-driven fan is, however, a necessity. Very few cars are of the air-cooled type, dispensing entirely with a water-cooling system.

The lubrication system of a motor car engine is so immensely important that oil can truly be said to be its life blood. It is surprising how few motorists realise that the automobile engine is an extremely delicate mechanism, and that the margin between perfection and the scrap heap is almost unbelievably fine. An engine can truthfully be said to be " worn out " when a thin film of metal is worn off every working part ; it may not be appreciated how very thin that film needs to be. If a mere two-thousandths

of an inch of metal—the thickness of a thin sheet of paper—
were removed from every bearing surface, the engine
would definitely be scrap.

All that stands between the various working surfaces of a
car's power unit, separating them and preventing them from
rasping themselves to destruction, is a film of oil—and
not a very thick film at that. It may be a thousandth of an
inch thick, but is usually less—and yet, if that film breaks
down, even for a brief moment, parts, revolving or moving
at high speed, would come into metal-to-metal contact.
The result would be scoring of surfaces, and " seizing," or
gripping and scarifying, and the parts would in all probabil-
ity be damaged beyond repair. I mention this to make it
quite clear that oil is an essential component of an engine ;
although it must be renewed from time to time it must not
be regarded as an unimportant extra.

Engines vary in their demands upon oil, just as they differ
in type and compression ratio, position of valves and speed
of revolution. A racing car's engine, for instance, running
nearly all the time on full throttle, would perhaps be more
sensitive as to the actual composition of its lubricating oil
than an ordinary touring engine. Yet, even with the latter,
it is the poorest of poor economy to save a few s¹ illings by
buying oil of unknown brand or grade, merely b cause it is
" guaranteed " motor oil. It is quite true that, in an
emergency for instance, it is possible to take liberties and to
drive gently for a few miles with almost any oil in the sump,
but, if bad or unsuitable oil be left there for a length of
time, ill-effects will accrue which will cause irremediable
troubles in the more or less near future.

No other type of engine makes such exacting demands
upon its lubricant as does a motor car engine. The speed
and load vary from second to second : the lubricant must

flow freely when the engine is started up from cold, yet must not lose its qualities under the heat and stress of full throttle opening. But that is not all ; every gallon of petrol consumed by the engine produces, as the result of combustion, more than its own volume of water. When an engine is first started up on a cold day, some of this water may be seen issuing from the exhaust pipe in drops and as steam, but some of it forms acids which remain inside the engine, on the cylinder walls, causing corrosion that eats away, rather than wears away, the metal of the cylinder.

When the engine reaches its normal working temperature, this water ceases to be harmful, for it is formed into dry, superheated steam, but another deleterious process starts work, and that is corrosion caused by oxygen. Oxygen acts more quickly on iron at high temperatures than it does under ordinary atmospheric temperatures, and, as it is always present in the gas made by the carburettor from petrol and air, it becomes mixed up with the oily fog which exists inside the engine all the time it is running. Its effect upon the oil is to form a sludge which can easily choke oil passages and pipes, and prevent the lubricant from reaching its intended points ; the sludge also tends to hold particles of grit and circulate them to the bearings. The efforts of technicians connected with the big oil concerns have been to evolve oils compounded to special formulæ which will overcome all the defects mentioned, hence the importance of strictly following the recommendations of the car manufacturer in regard to lubricating oil, and not thinking that any " motor oil " is as good as another.

A filter is, of course, incorporated in the lubrication system of practically every car, and much ingenuity has been devoted to developing special types of filter which prevent particles of solid material remaining in the oil-flow system. In the base of the engine, there is always a suction oil filter, through which must pass every drop of oil that enters the pump, to be forced, as we have seen, to all the bearings. In most cases this consists of a cylinder of gauze surrounding the pump. There may also be a pressure-type filter fitted at some point in the circulation system which will have a filtering element inside that can be removed and either cleaned or replaced after so many thousand miles' running. It must be emphasised, however, that these filters, while they eliminate solid particles which would be harmful in bearings, etc., cannot eliminate harmful liquids which may have mixed with the oil, and therefore are not an entirely satisfactory alternative to the periodic draining off of oil in the sump and the replenishment with new oil of the correct grade.

On many cars, a gauge is fitted on the facia board which shows the driver the pressure at which oil is flowing through the oil circulation system. The usual pressure is in the region of 40 lbs. per sq. in. when the car is travelling at anything from eighteen to twenty m.p.h. upwards; it will drop to a few lbs. when the engine is idling. A slight variation in pressure is not of great importance, but, if the drop is considerable, or the needle fluctuates, the driver should sit up and take notice; he should, in fact, pull up and investigate. Let us examine the reason for the gauge and the method by which it operates.

We have seen that the oil contained in the sump of the engine is forced around a system of pipes and passages by a pump which is in action the whole time the engine is revolving. The pump consists of two toothed wheels in mesh, like gear wheels, and their action is to draw oil in and force it out in a continual stream. The faster the engine turns, naturally, the faster the pump rotates and the greater the pressure at which the oil is sent on its way. But a limit to the pressure is fixed by the designer of the engine, to avoid burst pipes and joints ; he does this by means of a valve with a spring-loaded release, like the safety valve on a steam engine.

The pressure gauge which the driver sees is connected to the pipe line through which the oil is circulating, and the fact that the needle points to so many pounds per square inch indicates that the pump is working and that there is oil in the sump. Pressure by itself, as shown on the gauge, does not necessarily mean that the oil is reaching the bearings and other places for which it is intended. If, for instance, a pipe is blocked, there will be no flow to the points served by it, although the pressure gauge may be indicating quite satisfactorily. Also, there may be only a little oil in the sump, but, as the pump is situated at the lowest point of the engine, even a small amount of oil will keep the pump supplied.

When the engine is cold, the gauge will show a higher pressure than that at which the safety—or pressure release —valve blows off normally, because all oils are thicker when cold, and the valve will not pass the thick oil through with sufficient rapidity to reduce the pressure. In any case, this higher pressure is required to pass the oil to the bearings as quickly as possible. After an engine has run many thousands of miles, the bearings become worn slightly, and oil can then escape more easily from the passages through which it is forced to them. The result will be that the pressure gauge will record a lower reading when the oil is hot and thin. It may then be desirable to use a somewhat thicker grade of oil than that recommended for the engine when new.

In any case, the point I would emphasise is that the oil

D

pressure gauge, while important as a signal to the driver when things are *not* all right, is not an infallible tell-tale that everything is in one hundred per cent. order with the lubrication system. It is no substitute for verification of the level of oil in the sump, which can only be ascertained from the dipstick, nor is it unnecessary to change the oil because the gauge is still recording pressure within the system. On some modern cars the oil pressure gauge has been replaced by a warning light, which flashes up when the lubrication system is not functioning properly.

The Electrical System of the Car

I have, up to now, referred in very casual terms to the electrical system of the car, mentioning that it supplies the spark which ignites the explosive mixture in the cylinder. So much depends on the system, however, that, before leaving the engine it will be as well to examine more fully the important part that electricity plays in a motor car.

The only man who made a car without any electrical apparatus on it was Gottlieb Daimler, way back in the very early days of mechanically-propelled vehicles, and he relied on a red-hot tube to ignite the gas and so cause the explosion inside the cylinder. " Tube " ignition, as it was called, went out of favour before the twentieth century dawned, and, since then, every internal combustion engine used on a road vehicle has been equipped with electric ignition. At first a magneto was used, but nowadays the same system which provides the current for the ignition also gives the power for the starter, the trafficators and the lights ; on some of the very newest models it likewise activates the folding hood and the windows. It is, however, never likely to become the prime mover—the actual driving force—of a touring car, unless some more efficient method of storing electricity than the present type of battery is found.

A battery is an absolute necessity, because a car would otherwise be "dead" once the engine had stopped. Another name for battery is "accumulator," which describes its function very well, because it accumulates electricity, and gives it off when required. This does not mean that electricity can be put into a container and kept there indefinitely, but it does imply that a battery will "store" a certain amount of current and deliver it when called upon, if—and let the motorist mark this carefully—looked after with a degree of regularity.

Every car is provided with a battery, and sad and sorry things they often are, after being neglected for any length of time. On some cars the battery is hidden away in an inaccessible place, but, even if out of sight, it must not be allowed to go out of mind. Although we will not go into deep technical detail, a battery consists of lead plates, coated with chemical compounds, which are immersed in a weak solution of sulphuric acid. When an electric current is passed into these plates, an alteration in their chemical composition takes place ; when the current stops flowing in, a reverse chemical action causes a similar electric current to flow out. A battery has a certain capacity, depending upon the size of the plates, and the number of them, and it will "store" only an amount of current compatible with that capacity. If it is old, or in bad condition, or deficient in "electrolyte" (acid solution), its capacity will be far below what it should normally be.

Batteries are inclined to be finicky things. They do not like being overcharged, or over-discharged. They hate their plates to be left high and dry through the electrolyte evaporating and not being topped up. (I ought to mention that the electrolyte is composed of certain proportions of sulphuric acid and distilled water ; it is only the latter which evaporates, causing the acid to become too strong in the solution, and topping-up is done by adding distilled water.) They are most annoyed if they are topped-up with tap water, and show their displeasure by gassing. They also like their terminals greased, otherwise they grow a white mass of sulphate around them to vent their spite. Yes, batteries can be most unpleasant creatures if you neglect them.

On the other hand, a battery will be (usually) a faithful servant if humoured. Its span of life is generally regarded as being two years, with a bit more for luck. How much more may well depend on the owner's ministrations. The first sign of decay will be that it will not hold its charge, and cannot turn the starter with much energy after standing for a day or two, or even overnight. There is not much that can be done when this sets in, and, to avoid being let down unexpectedly, a new battery has to be fitted.

The charging current for the battery is generated by the dynamo, which is driven from the engine, usually by a belt but sometimes by a silent chain. A dynamo works on the same principle as those which supply current to our house mains, and, once again, there is no need to delve into technicalities, since the motorist does not have to concern himself with theory. It is sufficient to know that the dynamo generates the current and sends it to the battery when the latter requires it ; when fully charged, the automatically-operated regulator on the dynamo cuts down current output to deal only with the amount required for ignition.

There is, on many cars, a meter dial on the facia board which shows whether the dynamo is functioning, and the rate at which it is sending current to the battery. Often this gauge indicates that little or no current is passing, and that should be when the battery, being fully charged, is refusing any more. As, however, the meter—ampere meter, as it is usually called—is not of great importance so long as the dynamo is in working order, there is a tendency to eliminate it, and to rely on the ignition warning light to indicate this. The ignition light is so arranged that, when the switch is turned on, with engine dead, it glows red, but extinguishes itself when the dynamo takes the load off the battery, which it should do at about ten m.p.h. on top gear. Thereafter, so long as the engine is running, the ignition light should remain extinguished, only lighting up again when the engine speed drops so low that the dynamo ceases to generate sufficient current to maintain the ignition load.

The various services on the car which require electricity receive their supply from a distribution box, which is generally placed in the engine compartment, and accessible by lifting the bonnet. Each of the several circuits has its own fuses, which are of special type and can quickly be replaced by means of spring clip holders. One service, however, does not take its current from this centre, because it requires such a heavy supply ; this is the starter motor. It draws direct from the battery, via a special type of switch which brings on the load by magnetic action. The object of this is to give the starter motor a gentle start and to make the two gear wheels which have to be brought into engagement in order to turn the engine do so with as little snatch as possible.

When, therefore, you press or pull the starter control knob on the instrument panel, the effect is for the electricity from the battery to be switched on to the starter motor in sufficient strength to cause it to rotate. The motor shaft

is provided with a screw thread, and, at the end of this is a
small gear wheel. A spring holds this gear wheel in its
normal position, out of mesh with the large toothed ring
that surrounds the engine flywheel, until the motor starts
spinning. Immediately it does so, however, the screw
thread "winds" the small gear wheel along the shaft,
drawing it into engagement with the flywheel teeth. Once
the two sets of gears are meshed, the motor is turned full
on, and develops enough power to rotate the engine shaft.
If ever you have occasion to turn the engine by means of
the starting handle, you will understand that the motor
must be quite a powerful one to do the work !

In point of fact, a starter motor may have to develop as
much as one horse-power to do its job effectively, and, in
cold weather when the engine is stiff because the oil inside
it is congealed, perhaps more than that. If you have any
knowledge of electricity, you will understand that a motor
which develops one horse-power demands a current of the
order of 760 watts, and that, a watt being the product of
amperes multiplied by volts, and the car having an electrical
system of twelve, or perhaps only six, volts, the amperes
must be sixty and more in the former case, and double that
with a six-volt set.

For those who have no knowledge at all about electricity,
I should mention that currents of the amperage stated are
definitely of the " heavy " order. For a battery (or accumulator) to deliver them is a serious tax on its capacity and on
its construction. It amounts to this, that the use of the
starter is to overload, or overstrain, the battery, and, while
the types of battery used on cars are designed with full
regard to this overloading, the fact remains that excessive
use of the starter does positively weaken the battery and
bring on premature decay.

When I say "excessive" use of the starter, I mean prolonging the length of time the motor is in operation. If the car engine is in proper order, it should start up readily, even when cold, and the starter control should not have to be pressed, or pulled, for more than a brief period. When warm, the process should be practically instantaneous. Such short calls upon the battery's capacity, so far as overload is concerned, are not harmful to it. When, however, the starter is allowed to grind away for second after second, the effect rapidly becomes detrimental to the battery's plates. They tend to buckle in a desperate attempt to touch one another and so relieve their agony, and the chemical "paste" with which they are coated shrinks and is apt to loosen itself. Such damage can never be put right, and therefore the car-owner who values his battery's life will treat his starter with a good deal of respect. He will follow the probable recommendation of the maker of his engine and fill the sump with a thinner grade of oil in the winter ; he will perhaps bring himself to free the oil seal around pistons and in bearings, which has settled in during the night, by turning the engine over with the starting handle before operating the starter motor—it is this first movement of the working parts, breaking the oil film on a bitterly cold morning, which imposes undue strain on the motor and battery.

The wiring of the car's electrical system is complicated, and few motorists consider themselves competent to meddle with it. The great majority of British-made cars are fitted with Lucas electrical equipment, of which the makers— Joseph Lucas, Ltd., of Birmingham—are anxious to provide service facilities of a universally efficient nature. In most large centres of population, therefore, a service depot maintained from the factory is to be found, and the plan of supplying replacement units for all the major components in the system has been adopted. The majority of car-owners will find it quicker and more satisfactory to have a new unit fitted when any item gives trouble than to endeavour to get a repair effected to a faulty part of the system.

The only things with which a motorist need really concern himself are lamp bulbs and fuses. The former are of several different types and there may be two or three varieties on any one car. It is accordingly wise to carry a spare bulb of each type in some safe place on the car, and to familiarise oneself with the manner in which they are fitted to their respective lamps, since replacement may have to be undertaken in the dark. A good rule is to stow a torch away somewhere on the car, for it will sooner or later be a godsend to have it available. A small torch can easily be clipped along the steering column where it will be out of sight and out of mind until needed.

Fuses on the car serve just the same purpose as their equivalent in the house-lighting system; they are a sort of safety valve which will blow when the pressure becomes too great. The type fitted in a car-lighting set has the fusible wire encased in a glass tube. The ends of the tube are provided with copper ferrules, which are gripped in spring clips. When a fuse blows you may find that the trafficators do not work, or the interior roof light, and the reason may be that a short-circuit has occurred through a wire chafing and fouling some part of the metal bodywork. If a new fuse is fitted in this condition, it will merely blow immediately, so, before placing one in position and risking it, make an examination for some obvious fault and, if found, rectify it.

The demands that the modern car makes upon the battery and electrical system are ever growing. All the more reason, therefore, for acquiring a degree of respect for this servant of the motorist, who can be a very awkward customer if flouted or ignored. Perhaps one of the greatest insurances that the owner can easily take out is a trickle charger for the battery, which will keep the battery up to concert pitch. A trickle charger is a piece of apparatus permanently fitted in the garage ; it takes current from the mains and turns it into the sort of current that a battery likes, feeding it in small doses to its " patient " overnight so that the latter starts the next day full of pep. A battery which is in general good health prefers long, slow continuous charging, of the kind that a trickle charger gives, but, at the same time, a run-down battery that is not suffering from any defect in its plates can be charged fast, on special apparatus, in a few hours if required. Such treatment must, however, be applied by specialists who thoroughly understand what they are about.

The sparking plug is an essential part of the car's electrical system, and we have already noted that its important function is to ignite the explosive mixture inside the cylinder, at the moment of maximum compression. Most plugs look alike, at a casual glance, but there are many different types and so it is important that, when fitting a new set, the right pattern should be obtained. Just as in the case of lubricating oil, so with plugs the recommendation of the car manufacturer should be adopted.

Plugs are made with varying " reaches," the underlying principle being that the points at which the spark occurs should be brought to the correct point in relation to the interior of the cylinder head. Too long a reach may bring the points out into the full fury of the exploding gas, heating them to such an extent that they burn away or at least retain so much excess of heat that they spontaneously

D*

explode the charge before the spark is timed to perform that operation. On the other hand, if the reach is insufficient, the points may be shrouded in a pocket and give inadequate ignition. The correct reach would be, in most engines, for the points to be more or less flush with the interior wall of the combustion chamber.

One other important factor in a plug concerns what is known as its heat characteristic. This is the degree to which any particular engine causes its sparking plugs to acquire heat, due to the location relative to the valves that the plug is designed to occupy. As will be readily appreciated, a plug which has its points adjacent to the inlet valve will be cooled by the incoming gaseous charge to a greater extent than another where the points lie in the path of the flaming gas as it is exhausted from the cylinder. Again, one design of induction system may allow liquid petrol to reach the plug points, especially when starting, while another may leave the plug always dry of petrol, but may permit lubricating oil to drench it.

Because of these differences in engine design it is necessary to have sparking plugs of types which cater for the varying conditions. There are, normally, three such types, which are known as " cold," " soft " and " normal." The first would be suitable for a hot-running engine and the last for one that was not prone to overheat the plugs or which was prone to oiliness. The intermediate " normal " plug would suit an engine that had no special peculiarities. The main difference would be in the design of the points and the insulating shroud which is the basic feature of every sparking plug. It may be made of ceramic material or mica, generally the former. Nowadays porcelain is less used than it was before synthetic ceramics came into the range of practicability. The latter are almost always made of aluminium oxide which has been ground very finely, turned into a paste and then "sintered" (fused at a very high temperature). The metal electrodes are often of nickel and sometimes of platinum; they must, obviously, resist burning and oxidation. Some plugs have three points and some only one, but no matter how many "spark gaps" there may be, if any one of them becomes short-circuited by a fragment of burnt oil or other matter, none of the other gaps will continue to fire the engine—in other words, the plug has become "sooted up" and must be cleaned.

With some types of plug the central portion is made detachable so that the process of cleaning may be more easily done after taking the plug to pieces; the drawback, however, is that a detachable plug has to have a joint which can be kept thoroughly gas-tight. The modern tendency is to make plugs with a permanent sealing and for them to be thrown on the scrap heap when they have lived their useful life. It is a fact that a set of new plugs often acts like a tonic on an engine in a manner that no amount of cleaning of old plugs can effect.

The width of the gap between the points of a plug is important. A very wide gap may produce a larger spark, and it may have a beneficial effect on combustion at small throttle openings, as when idling or pulling slowly. At the same time, the ordinary type of coil may not develop sufficient electrical tension to maintain the heavier duty imposed by a wide gap. On racing cars, where the most intense spark possible is desired, special high-voltage coils are usually fitted to keep a wide gap in full operation; with the average touring car it is often doubtful whether there is any practical advantage to be gained from using a gap wider than the car manufacturer recommends. This is generally about .02 inch, and suits both starting up and ordinary fast running as well as the intermediate speeds.

Some Queries to Ask Yourself at this Point

1.—What is meant by " internal combustion " as applied to engines ?

2.—When an engine is said to run on petrol, to what process is the liquid petrol submitted in order to make it suitable for going into the engine ?

3.—What is the meaning of " to carburet " ?

4.—Run through the sequence of operations known as the " Otto cycle."

5.—How does a two-stroke engine differ from a four-stroke ?

6.—What constitutes the principle of a Diesel engine ? Also a gas turbine ?

7.—What causes the spark at the points of the sparking plug ?

8.—How is the heat generated by the internal combustion dissipated ?

9.—What part is played by the lubrication system ? Can you describe the process ?

10.—What makes the valves go up and down ?

11.—What is meant by " high compression " ?

12.—How is the spark advanced, and why ?

13.—What causes an engine to " pink " ?

14.—What is meant by a " flexible " engine ?

15.—Can you describe the passage of the exhaust gas from cylinder to atmosphere ? Why is a motor car engine less noisy than that of a motor cycle ?

16.—What is meant by " thermo-syphon " cooling ?

17.—How thick would a film of lubricating oil be inside a bearing ?

18.—Why must a motorist always be careful of the oil he puts in his engine ?

19.—What causes corrosion inside an engine ?

20.—Is there any alternative to electricity for igniting the explosive charge inside the cylinder ?

The Transmission

The power which the engine develops in the form of a rotary movement, which is nearly always in a line parallel with the chassis frame of the car, has to be transformed into an urge imparted to the road wheels, which can make them rotate in both forward and reverse direction, and, at the will of the driver, at any required speed. Also, it must be capable of setting them in motion from standstill. To achieve this end, a transmission system is needed which can couple the source of power to the road wheels in a positive manner, yet one which is capable of considerable variation.

I have already outlined the several components embodied on a car whereby the desired result is obtained. I mentioned that there is a clutch to form the friction link which permits the engine, already running, to start stationary wheels into motion and that a gearbox provides a choice of several alternative ratios between engine and road wheel speeds. I also pointed out that the differential gear incorporated in the driving axle enables the two wheels, coupled apparently rigidly to the one shaft, to revolve at varying speeds. Let us now consider in detail the mechanics of these essential links in the transmission chain.

We will deal first with the clutch because that is the component which enters first into the sequence of operations. It is usually located immediately behind the engine, and often forms one piece with it, at least as regards its casing. In fact, the flywheel of the engine is generally pressed into service to constitute one surface of the clutch and thereby to eliminate using a separate plate for it. The action is simply explained by imagining a flat, smooth plate (the surface of the flywheel) spinning round, and a similar plate being pressed into contact with it. The natural effect would be for the moving plate to exercise friction on the stationary one and, as the friction increased, for the motion to be imparted from one to the other until when both were revolving at the same speed, they would move around as one.

That does, in fact, describe accurately the operation of every clutch fitted to a motor car. The only variation is found in the means whereby the plates are pressed into contact, also the type of material used for the plates and for lining one of them in order to let the friction be applied in the smoothest and most efficient manner, or, in the case of " fluid transmission," to cause the motion of one to be imparted to the other without there being any physical contact between the metal portions of the clutch.

To deal with the normal, or non-fluid, type of clutch first, it consists of a spring-loaded plate which is capable of moving longitudinally on a shaft projecting from the front end of the gearbox. In other words, it can slide along this shaft, without being able to revolve unless it carries the shaft round with it. This is usually effected by cutting keyways, or splines as they are called, on the shaft, with grooves to match in the centre of the plate. There is a device at the back of the plate, and integral with it, by means of which the plate may be made to slide backwards on the shaft when the pedal under the driver's left foot is pressed, also a strong spring which automatically presses the plate forward along the shaft so long as the driver is not pushing on his pedal.

The normal position for the sliding plate is, therefore, hard up against the flywheel, pressed into engagement with it by virtue of the spring's heavy pressure. In this position, any rotatory movement of the flywheel is bound to be transmitted to the clutch plate, and, because of the splines and grooves in shaft and plate, to cause the shaft projecting from the front end of the gearbox to be carried round too. Let the driver push down his clutch pedal, however, and the movement transmitted by the device at the back of the clutch plate causes the plate to be slid back along the shaft, compressing the spring in the process by breaking the friction engagement between the flywheel and the clutch plate. In motor car parlance, the clutch is now " out."

Let us see the action as the clutch goes " in." The driver, by gently relaxing pressure on the pedal, allows the sliding plate to be brought gradually forward by the spring pressure until it is forced up against the smooth surface of the flywheel. If the latter is rotating, the tendency will naturally be for the sliding plate to be dragged round, but whether the flywheel will be able to do this depends upon the power that is behind it. As we have seen, the power of a motor-car engine grows with the speed of its rotation, and so the driver will have to " feel," as he lets in the clutch, whether he is giving the engine sufficient throttle to enable it to impart motion to the stationary clutch plate, or, in other words, to start the car into motion.

The process of letting in the clutch naturally engenders heat, caused by the friction set up between the clutch plates. If they were both made of the same metal—steel, for instance—there would be a great possibility of the two surfaces " seizing " because of this heat, unless lubricant were provided to guard against this. Formerly, clutches did consist of metal-to-metal contact of this kind, and they ran in an oilbath, but it became realised that there were practical advantages in using dry surfaces, and so the practice of utilising a lining for the sliding plate, which would remain unaffected by heat and friction yet would afford a good, slip-free contact once fully " in," attained widespread favour and is the most generally used type of clutch on modern cars.

In spite of the efficiency of clutch linings, however, which are composed of similar material to the linings of brake shoes, it is detrimental to impose too much heat-producing slipping on them. When the clutch is let in, the action of the driver's operation of the pedal should be smooth yet determined ; he should " rev up " the engine just sufficiently to make it develop a sufficiency of power in comparison with the load (i.e., the car may be standing on an upgrade, in which case the load is greater than when on the level), and then should feed the clutch in without hesitation, so that the friction caused by engagement quickly ceases. He should select the right gear for starting off, using bottom if the load is great and the next higher gear only if the car is standing on a down gradient. The higher the gear in which the car is started off, the greater will be the load on the engine and, accordingly, the more slipping the clutch will have to be given in getting under way.

In the case of a " fluid " flywheel, the type of clutch as detailed above is eliminated, and the motion of the rotating engine is transmitted to the propeller shaft by the dragging action of oil or fluid contained in the " clutch " housing. The word clutch is not employed, but the fact remains that the action is entirely similar. Imagine two turbine blades (the uninitiated may think of them as glorified fans) being contained in a leakproof casing, the two sets of blades being separated by a very minute distance—all but touching, in fact. So long as the casing remains empty, the two turbines can revolve quite independently of one another; when, however, the casing is filled with a fluid, the action is that movement of one set of blades tends to be transmitted to the other. The fluid is, in fact, forced against the vanes of the second turbine and, when the pressure set up reaches a sufficient value, or strength, it will cause this turbine to rotate. If you imagine a jet of water directed upon the blades of a stationary electric fan you will immediately realise how a fluid flywheel works. The same principle is, of course, used in steam turbines, or in hydro-electric generators.

If, therefore, we compare a fluid flywheel with a normal type of clutch, we see that there is very much the same sort of friction action, except that fluid is taking the place of the clutch lining and there is no direct contact between the component plates. That friction *is* caused is made obvious by the fact that the fluid heats up considerably if the fluid flywheel is made to " slip " while under load, and the nature of the exact fluid employed has to be carefully computed. It is not merely oil, for it must be sufficiently liquid to avoid drag when the car is at rest and the engine idling, yet it must be sufficiently viscose to prevent any undue amount of slip when full load is being transmitted. Owners of cars fitted with this type of transmission must, therefore, be most particular to use only the recommended fluid.

A fluid flywheel is not to be confused with hydraulic transmission, of the type now gaining popularity on the other side of the Atlantic. It is true that such transmissions do incorporate turbine blades actuated by hydraulic pressure, but a fluid flywheel cannot be used as a complete transmission, i.e., without embodying a gearbox to make definite reduction, or variation, of gear ratio as between

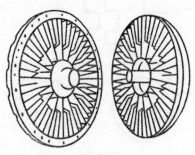

FIG. 29

The component parts of a fluid flywheel. They work in close proximity to one another, and fluid forms the only " coupling " between them.

engine and road wheels. The reason for this is that the fluid heats up, as already mentioned, when " slip " sets in, and nothing but slip can cause a variation in gear ratio when a fluid flywheel alone is being considered. Hydraulic transmission, superseding as it does both the clutch or fluid flywheel and the gearbox, will undoubtedly make great progress, but it is at present best suited to a car with large engine and not to one of normal British type.

A general description of the manner in which a gearbox operates has already been given. The modern tendency is for the actual gear wheels to remain in constant mesh, being coupled to the transmission as required by means of what are known as " dog clutches." These are best described as being projections which engage with recesses, and, when once in engagement, provide a positive (i.e., non-slipping) drive from one to another.

DOG CLUTCH

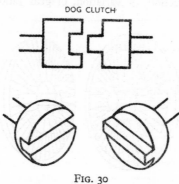

FIG. 30
The principle of a " dog clutch."

The action of moving the gear lever is to cause what are known as selectors to be moved inside the gearbox. There is one selector for every pair of gears, and, when the driver shifts the gear control from one position to another, he causes a motion to be transmitted through the operating mechanism which first returns the selector in use to the neutral position, where no gears are engaged, and then engages with the selector actuating the pair of gears next desired, bringing the dog clutches together and meshing them. For instance, if changing up from second to third gear, the movement of the gear lever would be first to disengage the dog clutch holding second gear in mesh and next to enter the forked end of third gear selector, pushing this in the direction that caused it to make the appropriate dog clutch engage.

The foregoing description applies to the " normal " type of gearbox, of which the engineer Panhard remarked, more than half-a-century ago, " It works, but it is brutal." The application of synchro-mesh has, however, removed much of the brutality from the meshing of the gears, to which Panhard was referring. Until synchro-mesh came into use, the gear wheels themselves were slid into mesh, and an unskilful driver might make the most appalling noises when he tried to engage the teeth of two wheels which were rotating at very different speeds.

Synchro-mesh, as the name implies, causes synchronisation of the meshing gears, or, as we have seen, dog clutches. If we think of the friction clutch as being a piece of mechanism which makes two surfaces rotate at the same speed, and then imagine each pair of gears being provided with clutches which come into engagement before the wheels, or dog clutches, themselves do, bringing speeds to the same, so that the meshing portions come together in harmony, we have appreciated what synchro-mesh really is. It has undoubtedly given the normal gearbox a new lease of life in the hands of the public.

The only serious challenger to it throughout the years of motoring has been the epicyclic gear, with or without pre-selector. This is another form of constant-mesh gearbox, and the dictionary definition of " epicyclic " gives a clue to its construction : it is " a small circle whose centre is situated on the circumference of a greater circle." If the greater circle is provided with teeth around its internal circumference, and small gear wheels mesh with this internally-toothed ring, the axes (plural of axis) on which these gear wheels revolve will themselves revolve at a slow rate if the large wheel drives the little ones round. If, however, you lock the little wheels so they cannot revolve, the whole assembly, big wheel and little wheels and axes all together, will revolve at the same speed as the big wheel. Here you have the simplest form of epicyclic two-speed

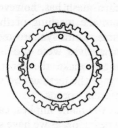

FIG. 31

An epicyclic gear has internally toothed large gear wheels and small pinions meshing continuously. Variation in speed is obtained by locking certain assemblies of gears.

gear, exactly as Henry Ford used on his original " Model T," commonly known as the " Tin Lizzie."

From that simple start epicyclic gearboxes for motor cars have developed into highly sophisticated pieces of mechanism providing four ratios. Many buses and coaches have them, too, and they were used on armoured vehicles in the last war, so they can be regarded as perfectly reliable and satisfactory. Their construction, broadly speaking, is on similar lines to those just described, the required gear ratio being brought into action by locking one set or another of meshing gear wheels to make the rest of the assembly revolve at the desired relative speed. Where pre-selection is incorporated, movement of the gear lever merely makes the preparatory choice of the ratio next to be brought into use, the actual changing being effected by the driver pushing down the left pedal, which would normally be the clutch pedal. An " automatic " clutch, either operated by centrifugal force* or by fluid transmission, is always used in conjunction with a pre-selective epicyclic gearbox.

From the gearbox, of whatever type it may be, there is a propeller shaft to form the connecting link with the driving axle and the road wheels. This propeller shaft is not just a straight rod, or tube, which can be held down in bearings like the propeller shaft of a steamship. It has to move up

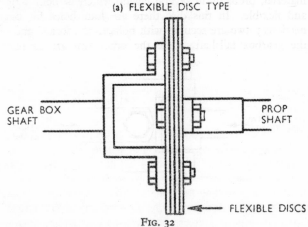

(a) FLEXIBLE DISC TYPE

GEAR BOX
SHAFT

PROP
SHAFT

FLEXIBLE DISCS

Fig. 32

A universal joint, as fitted at the front end of the propeller shaft. The flexible discs allow the propeller shaft and gearbox shaft to run out of line.

and down at its tail end in consonance with the movement of the road wheels and their springs ; also it has to vary its length very slightly because the oscillation of the axle due to spring movement causes a continual variation in the distance between gearbox and axle.

* Such a clutch is of normal type, but the operation is by centrifugal force, i.e., the faster it spins the harder the plates are pressed together, and vice versa.

At both ends of the propeller shaft, therefore, a special form of connection known as a universal joint has to be fitted. This enables the drive to be taken at an angle and for power to be transmitted continuously even though the propeller shaft may be rising and falling as the wheels roll over bumps and holes in the road surface. At the front end, the universal joint often consists of a disc of fabric (a special material, probably in several layers) which is both tough and flexible. In this disc there are four holes for connections; two are secured with bolts to the forked end of the gearbox tailshaft, while the other two are similarly

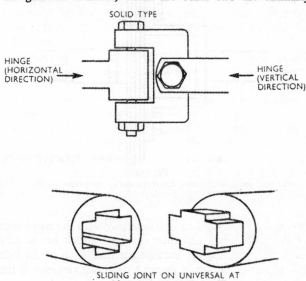

SOLID TYPE

HINGE (HORIZONTAL DIRECTION)

HINGE (VERTICAL DIRECTION)

SLIDING JOINT ON UNIVERSAL AT REAR END OF PROP SHAFT

FIG. 33

Metal-to-metal universal joint, with sliding portion, used at rear end of propeller shaft.

bolted to the forked front end of the propeller shaft. Movement of the latter is thus absorbed by the flexing of the fabric disc.

The universal joint at the back axle end of the propeller shaft, however, is generally of metal-to-metal construction, with a sliding member to allow of the lengthening and shortening of the distance the propeller shaft has to drive. This joint can best be likened to a double hinge, the effect of which is similar to that accomplished by the flexing of the fabric disc. There is naturally a tendency to some considerable amount of wear on a metal-to-metal universal joint, and a leather dust-cover is usually fitted to protect the sliding member; this has to be kept stuffed with grease. The exact type of universal joints fitted varies with different makes of car.

The back axle receives its driving force from the propeller shaft at a point which is generally midway between the road wheels, although this is not necessarily so, and transforms the rotatory movement which, up to now, has been parallel with the chassis frame, to one that is at right-angles to it. This is effected through the medium of one of two types of gearings; the first, and most generally employed, is what is known as bevel and the other is worm. Let us briefly examine both of them.

Bevel gearing is so called because the teeth of the gear wheels are formed at an angle, and the smaller of the pair has the appearance of a bevelled-off cone. On the large wheel the teeth are cut so that everyone of them radiates from the centre of the wheel, the arrangement of them being such that they lie on the same plane as the side of the gear wheel, and not on its outside edge as in the case of gearbox wheels. When the bevel wheels are paired, therefore, the smaller one lies along the larger one and the angle formed by the bevel of the smaller would, if the lines were produced, have its apex in the centre of the large wheel.

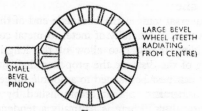

LARGE BEVEL
WHEEL (TEETH
RADIATING
FROM CENTRE)

SMALL
BEVEL
PINION

FIG. 34
Diagrammatic illustration of a bevel gear.

The propeller shaft drives the smaller wheel, which carries the large one round at a speed relative to the ratio of size between the pair. This relationship is known as the " final drive ratio," and determines the actual gearing between engine and road wheels when on top gear, i.e., when there is a direct drive through the gearbox and both its input and output shafts are revolving at the same speed. Many car manufacturers vary this final drive ratio, suiting it to conditions in the territory to which the car is being dispatched when it leaves the factory. Thus, one which is destined for mountainous or rough country overseas may have a lower final drive ratio than one which is going to a country or district where the road conditions are good, and mainly flat. Expert drivers entering for trials and rallies pay great attention to their final drive ratio, and may change the axle in order to secure one which they consider will give the car an advantage in some arduous test.

Such a course is not possible for the ordinary owner-driver, nor would he ever be likely to wish to do so. I mention the matter, however, merely to indicate that the back axle has it own particular effect on the gearing of a car. The usual ratio for the final drive will be somewhere between four and five to one, i.e., the propeller shaft will revolve that number of times to every once of the shaft which drives the road wheels. This is equivalent to saying that top gear is four or five to one, or whatever may be the exact ratio of the back axle's gearing. A motor car manufacturer aims to give as high a top gear as is consistent with the engine being able to furnish good acceleration and general performance on top gear; the higher the gear, within reason, the better the petrol consumption.

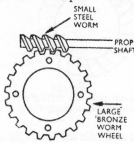

SMALL STEEL WORM

PROP SHAFT

LARGE BRONZE WORM WHEEL

FIG. 35
Diagrammatic illustration of worm gearing. The worm may be above or below the large bronze wheel.

Worm gearing receives its name from the "worm," or screw thread, which constitutes the driving unit of the gear. This is made of hardened steel, the large wheel which it drives being of bronze. The latter is usually a thick ring with teeth cut on the periphery, and bolted to the steel retainers of the differential cage. As the worm revolves, it "screws" the big wheel round, and this, like the bevel wheel, is the more slowly rotating member which drives the road wheels.

Two advantages are claimed for worm drive; the first is

that it is ordinarily very quiet because the large wheel is made of bronze. The second is that, if the small driving worm is placed at the bottom of the axle, the line of the propeller shaft is low and the floor of the car can be flat. The latter advantage is also shared by what is known as the "hypoid" bevel axle in which the small bevel wheel is placed below the centre of the large bevel wheel. This naturally requires a special formation for the teeth of the

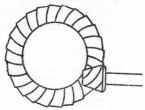

FIG. 36

With a " hypoid " bevel gear, the driving pinion is below the centre line of the large bevel wheel, allowing the propeller shaft to be set lower.

bevel gears and it also calls for special lubricant to be used in the axle casing, because the load placed on the gear wheels is increased and the friction between them also becomes greater. "Hypoid"-type axles are, however, commonly used in modern cars.

The differential gear, which is interposed between the bevel or worm gear and the shafts which do the actual driving of the wheels (these are known as the "half-shafts"), lies within the driven unit, i.e., the large wheel, of the axle. Its principle can easily be understood if one imagines that, inside that large wheel, there is a bar going straight across on which are mounted two small bevel wheels, these being free to revolve on the bar. A further bevel wheel mounted rigidly on each half-shaft meshes with those two wheels, so that we have four small bevel wheels, all the same size, forming one complete unit in

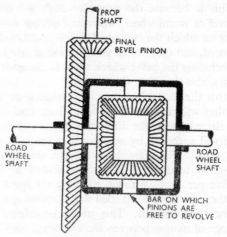

FIG. 37

A diagrammatic illustration of the differential gear, showing the four small bevel pinions which form a complete assembly and allow the road wheels to revolve at varying speeds.

continuous engagement. Now imagine the stationary car jacked up at the back so that both wheels are clear of the ground. If one of those wheels is turned by hand the motion will be transmitted to the bevel wheel fixed to the inner end of its half-shaft. This will cause the two bevel wheels, mounted on the crossbar, to follow suit. Their movement will be passed on to the bevel wheel fixed to the half-shaft which drives the *other* road wheel, so that this, also, will be set in motion—but in the reverse direction to the first one which is being turned.

If we now start up the engine, still with the road wheels

jacked up, and engage a gear (any one) and then let the clutch in, *both* the wheels will rotate, and in the same direction. This is because the propeller shaft is driving the small bevel or worm wheel, which is carrying round with it the bar on which the two small differential bevel wheels are mounted, and they are all going round as one complete whole, including the bevel wheels fixed to the ends of both half-shafts, also the road wheels.

Note that the road wheels are both rotating at the same speed ; they will continue to do so until the load on one of them is altered, when the differential gears will come into play and will speed up by an equivalent amount the free-running wheel. For example, if a brake were applied to the left-hand road wheel so that it slowed it by, say, twenty-five per cent., without affecting the speed of the engine, then the right-hand road wheel would speed itself up by the same amount. This would be effected by an interchange of motion between the two small bevel wheels revolving on the bar.

We can thus see why, when a car rounds a corner, the differential gear allows the inner wheel to run slower than the outer one. The friction between road and tyre in the case of the former constitutes a brake and sets the outer wheel revolving faster, which it is being urged to do by road friction ; hence the necessary relative adjustment of speed is effected and the car travels smoothly round the bend with the two back wheels both driving but revolving at widely different speeds. The differential can equally prove itself a nuisance when the car gets one wheel into a patch of grease or ice on the roadside, for, if there is no grip for its tyre, the differential will allow it to spin gaily and to deprive the other wheel of any driving force whatsoever.

We have thus traced the transmission of power developed by the engine right through the car from the time it enters, so to speak, the clutch to the time it leaves the back wheels, in the form of turning effort applied to the road through the tyres. One point that should perhaps be mentioned is that reverse motion is obtained by means of an extra train of gear wheels in the gearbox ; one additional pinion (gear wheel) interposed between the two shafts is brought into play by the driver moving the gear lever into reverse position and causes the motion of the driven shaft to be in the opposite direction. Reverse gear is always of very low ratio, usually lower than bottom speed in the forward direction.

So far we have considered the transmission only from the aspect of it driving the car. When, however, the driver takes his foot off the accelerator and thereby cuts off the engine's power, the road wheels become the driving force and they transmit the power derived from the car's momentum to the engine via the propeller shaft and the gearbox. Naturally, a considerable amount of power is needed to rotate a " dead " engine, which thus acts as a brake. This effect is magnified if one of the intermediate gears is engaged, by the driver changing down from top to third or second. When commencing the descent of a long and steep hill it is good practice to do this, for much wear on the brakes can thereby be avoided. The engine should *not* be switched off, as there may be sooting-up of the sparking plugs if this is done, due to oil being sucked up past the pistons into the combustion chambers. If the ignition is left switched on, however, the sparking-plug points are kept clean by the passage of the electric sparks.

There was at one period a tendency to fit a freewheel in the transmission so that, when the driver let the accelerator come up, the car would " coast " without having to rotate the engine. There were, possibly, advantages to be gained from this practice in the matter of petrol consumption because the car's momentum could be used freely whenever hills were descended, even quite minor ones. The free-wheel for cars has not gained in popularity with the passage of years, however, and at the time of writing there remains only one make of car which continues to fit the device. None the less, many drivers do indulge in " coasting " down suitable hills, and there is no harm done to the car if the gear lever is put into neutral and the foot taken off the clutch pedal. The engine must be left idling, and, just before the gear lever is put back into the top gear position the engine is speeded up by a touch on the accelerator so that, when the clutch pedal is quickly pressed and the gear engaged, the engine will be running at about the required speed relative to the pace at which the car is " coasting." It is, however, the worst possible practice to " coast " by pressing the clutch pedal down and holding it there, for serious wear will quickly ensue in the clutch withdrawal mechanism.

Suspension

Every car has to have springing of some sort or another to insulate the passengers, and the mechanism, from shocks set up by the passage of the wheels over inequalities in the road surface. From the very beginning motor engineers have borrowed the " leaf " type of spring from the horse carriage, and for at least forty years it was practically universal for both front and back axles to be mounted on semi-elliptic leaf springs. These consisted, of course, of a series of leaves made of spring steel, held together by a central bolt and having the bottom leaf rolled over at each

end to form an eye through which the shackle bolt passed
to secure the spring to the chassis.

Even to-day the same semi-elliptic leaf-spring system is
still in service, at any rate for the rear axle. On many
modern cars the front wheels are fitted with what is termed
" independent springing," whereby they may respond to

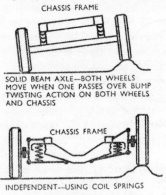

CHASSIS FRAME

SOLID BEAM AXLE—BOTH WHEELS
MOVE WHEN ONE PASSES OVER BUMP
TWISTING ACTION ON BOTH WHEELS
AND CHASSIS

CHASSIS FRAME

INDEPENDENT—USING COIL SPRINGS

FIG. 38

*This diagram indicates the difference between a solid-beam axle and
independent front-wheel suspension.*

road shocks independently of one another. When the front
axle was of the solid beam type they naturally had to work
in unison. Furthermore, the weight of the solid beam of the
axle was unsprung, and engineers are always anxious to
reduce unsprung weight to the greatest possible extent in
order to improve the riding qualities of a car.

The springing medium, when independent front-wheel
suspension is fitted, may be of several types. It may, in the
first place, be a leaf spring, arranged transversely across the
chassis so that each end can flex separately from the other.
Spiral, or coil, springs are widely employed, one on either

side of the car, and torsion bars are likewise favoured by many motor manufacturers. The latter method usually embodies a long steel bar running parallel with the side members of the chassis : the rear end of the bar is firmly fixed to the chassis and the front end to the hinge-pin on

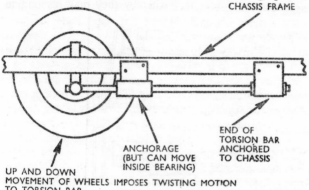

CHASSIS FRAME

END OF
TORSION BAR
ANCHORED
TO CHASSIS

ANCHORAGE
(BUT CAN MOVE
INSIDE BEARING)

UP AND DOWN
MOVEMENT OF WHEELS IMPOSES TWISTING MOTION
TO TORSION BAR

FIG. 39

Torsion-bar suspension is gaining popularity. It imposes a twisting strain on a steel bar and derives its springing action therefrom.

which the road wheel is mounted. As the latter moves up and down, a twisting effort is put upon the long bar and the steel of which it is made responds to it in the same way as does a flat piece of spring steel. Sometimes, indeed, flat strips of steel are used instead of a torsion bar, a series of them being built up in similar fashion to the leaf spring, but twisted under load instead of flexed. Or the torsion bar may be a steel tube. Pneumatic springing is also being experimented with and may in due course take its place alongside the other systems.

Whatever means be actually adopted to give the springing effect, some form of " damping " is necessary to prevent

E

rebound after the spring has been compressed. As is well known, the effort which is put in to compress a spring will be returned in full measure when the pressure is relaxed. A bump in the road which forced the wheel upwards and thereby compressed the springing medium would naturally have a reaction which, if not otherwise absorbed, might communicate a bouncing effect to the car's body.

To absorb spring reaction shock absorbers, or dampers, are fitted to the suspension of almost every car. Sometimes they are of friction type, with two flat surfaces lined with friction material moving over one another and offering resistance to liveliness. Others which are widely employed work on the hydraulic principle, the casing of the damper containing oil which has to be forced from one chamber to another through an aperture of small size. Many and various types of shock absorber are fitted by different car manufacturers, and upon their efficiency depends much of the comfort of the passengers' ride and also the road-holding characteristics of the vehicle as a whole.

The last is a highly important matter, for, in an emergency, if the driver cannot " hold " the car it may get into difficulties. Imagine, for instance, a car with too-lively springing hitting a bad bump when travelling at speed, especially if the driver had had to pull over to the side of the road to avoid other traffic. The rebound of the springs might easily cause the car to bounce and for the driver to lose control of the front wheels with disastrous results. On the other hand, too much damping, or snubbing, of the springs causes a car to ride harshly.

Brakes

Since braking on all four wheels came into general use (a development which took place in the early 1920s) the safety and certainty of handling of a car has become much greater. When every bit of brake power was applied to the rear wheels only, the possibility of skidding was infinitely greater than it is to-day. None the less, a car with powerful four-wheel brakes still demands a considerable amount of care to avoid a front-wheel skid on treacherous surfaces. It should be borne in mind that the major part of the braking effort is directed to the front wheels and that a locked front wheel puts a car completely out of control.

Most brake designs introduce what is known as " servo " action. This implies that the drag between brake shoes and brake drum, when pressure is applied to the brake pedal, sets up a tendency for the shoes to be carried round with the revolving drum. If the anchorage of the leading shoe is arranged so that this forces the trailing shoe into harder contact with the drum, a " self-wrapping," or servo, action is obtained which derives its power from the momentum of the car.

Servo action of this nature is utilised on many designs of braking system, while vacuum assistance is also used, especially on heavier types of vehicle. The principle of this latter is that the " suction," or lowering of pressure, in the induction pipe of the engine is employed to exhaust the air from a vacuum reservoir. When the brake pedal is pressed communication is opened between this and a cylinder containing a piston which is caused to move by the vacuum and, in so doing, exerts a pull on the brake gear. If the brakes have to be applied when the engine is not running and there is no vacuum in the cylinder, provision is made for over-riding control to be exercised by the driver's pedal.

Hydraulic operation is largely used for brake actuation. This means, in effect, that movement on the brake pedal is transmitted to the brake shoes by means of a column of liquid instead of a rod or cable. In other words, pressure of the driver's foot on the pedal causes liquid to be forced through pipes leading to each of the wheels where, inside the brake drum, the oil pressure is converted into movement of small pistons inside a cylinder; these pistons, being forced outwards, transmit their movement to the ends of the brake shoes. A reservoir of brake fluid is provided in the system to ensure that the mechanism is kept continually topped up.

The modern tendency is for the handbrake to be regarded purely as a parking brake and to operate on the rear wheels only. This is because braking systems have been given so much power by the development of " self-wrapping " and other servo devices that supplementary pressure, such as used to be demanded from the handbrake, is no longer of any practical value in bringing a car to a standstill, because it is the coefficient of friction between tyres and road which governs the maximum degree of retardation the brakes can exert.

Steering Gear

Movement of the steering wheel is transmitted to the front wheels in a variety of ways. One of the earliest methods, which is now returning to favour, is for there to be a rack and pinion at the foot of the steering column; the latter is, of course, the long rod or tube which has the steering wheel fixed to its upper end. A toothed pinion, or gear wheel, fixed to the lower end of the column, engages with a ratchet or rack which is caused to be moved sideways and, in so doing, carries with it a track rod connecting the two swivel arms that are attached to the front-wheel spindles.

Alternative methods of moving the track rod are to have a kind of gearbox on the steering column which converts the rotatory motion of the column into a push-and-pull movement of what is known as a drop arm. This works in a fore-and-aft path parallel with the chassis frame, and communicates its movement to one of the front-wheel swivel pins (or "king-pins" as they are termed). The other wheel receives its steering control by means of the track rod which passes transversely across the chassis.

Inside the steering gearbox the mechanism may consist of a worm and nut, or a cam and roller (the cam being like a curved thread cut in a round steel bar), but, whatever the design, the principal requirement is that the action shall be positive, shall not have much "backlash" and shall work freely and not become "sticky" after some considerable amount of use. Generally speaking, the average motorist will never need to know much about the interior of the steering gearbox on his car, for it is one of the parts that give the least trouble and require a minimum of attention.

On the other hand, the track rod is an item which needs to be understood and its bearing upon the important matter of tyre wear fully appreciated. It is this rod which keeps the front wheels in their path, and upon its adjustment depends the effect of that path on the front tyres. Let us examine this matter with some care, therefore, for owners driving identical makes of car on similar tyres can quite easily get mileages from them which vary very considerably. The subject is of more than usual interest, because cars of new design have now been on the road sufficiently long for the average owner to obtain some idea of how various designs of front-wheel suspension can affect tyre life, and his best way to lengthen this.

Results of careful tyre-wear observation carried out by one of the biggest manufacturers have revealed that, on any given make of car, the average tyre life that can be obtained varies over a range of six or seven to one. This is due to the influence of driving methods, weather, road conditions and all of these factors combined with design of chassis and maintenance given to tyres by the owner. Individual cases have given mileages as high as 35,000 and as low as 5,000 where mechanical factors have been very much of a muchness.

Generally speaking—although there are exceptions—all the factors responsible for unduly low or especially high tyre mileages are under the control of the driver. The relative importance of these various factors has, however, changed in the last few years. Whereas braking and acceleration probably headed the list there must now be taken into consideration, also, the influence of independent front-wheel suspension, the speed at which bends and curves are taken and the effect of continual driving at high average speed. There is one more difference, and that is that, whilst in the past wear was usually more pronounced on the rear-wheel tyres, to-day (in the case of independently-sprung cars) the wear is greater at the front.

The adverse effect on tyre wear attributable to independent front-wheel suspension arises mainly from the geometrical changes which inevitably occur as one or other of the front wheels rises and falls, also from the fact that the system permits of cornering at higher speeds and of faster driving over poor road surfaces without discomfort. I should perhaps add that the term " cornering " includes motoring along twisty roads and around traffic islands. When a car is steered out of a straight path, all tyres deviate from the direction in which the car is travelling, and this is not a defect in either driving method or chassis design, but is an essential thing to enable forces to be obtained from the tyres which will guide the car round the corner.

These are known as "cornering forces," and they are also necessary to control the course of a car on cambered roads or in a cross-wind. The nature of cornering force can perhaps be more readily understood if compared with the swinging of a weight on a piece of string. Centrifugal force will stretch the string tight, and, if the weight is heavy enough and the string is swung fast enough, centrifugal force will increase until the string breaks and the weight flies out of control. When a car corners, similar forces are operating but there is no string to keep the car under control : the equivalent is provided by cornering force set up within the tyres, which opposes the centrifugal force.

This cornering force is obtained from the front and rear tyres, which are moving in a slightly different direction to that in which the driver is steering. Natural reaction in the tyre is trying to recover from this distorted position, and, in doing so, the tyre tread must necessarily rub the surface of the road to a certain extent. It is this rubbing which is so potent a factor in wearing away the rubber, and obviously high cornering speeds intensify the rubbing effect. In this connection the report of an experiment conducted in America is of interest : a vacuum cleaner was employed to pick up samples of road dust on corners and on a straight stretch of road. When analysed for rubber content, the dust taken from the corner yielded eight times as much as the other sample !

This tyre deviation in cornering is not to be confused with

incorrect setting of the front wheels, which is governed by the adjustment of the screwed portion of the track rod, about which we have been talking earlier on. This adjustment secures the amount in which the front wheels " toe in " or " toe out," these expressions being used to denote the amount by which the wheels are out of parallel with the car at rest. It is usually necessary for there to be a certain degree of one or the other, for the reason that, when the car gets under way, the effect of springing, load and impact of the road may combine to have an effect on wheel setting which would make them run out of true if they were set to be exactly parallel when the car was stationary.

The amount of " toe in " or the reverse is a matter for the car manufacturer to decide, and his recommended setting should allow of the two front wheels being parallel when the car is moving in a straight line forward. It is generally known that too much " toe in " wears the left front tyre and too much " toe out " the right front tyre, on cars running according to the British rule of the road. This is because a car which is being driven on the left-hand side of the road is having to be " held " out of the nearside kerb by the steering, which is tantamount to saying that, in order to pursue a straightforward path, the car must be proceeding in a somewhat " crab "-like manner (diagram A). If the front wheels are " toed out " excessively (diagram B) the offside front wheel is being dragged along considerably out of its proper path, while, if " toed in " too much, it is the nearside tyre which is being maltreated (diagram C).

Sometimes the front-wheel tyres are prone to wear unevenly, and this is almost always due to the distribution of weight and braking power, also to the employment of independent front-wheel suspension. Tyres on driven

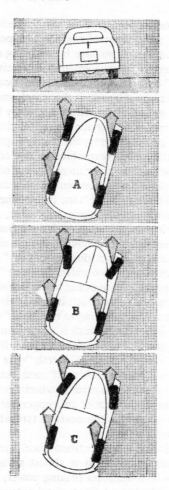

FIG. 40
This diagram illustrates the strain put upon tyres by driving on steeply cambered roads (top) or with incorrect setting of front wheels. In A the four wheels are parallel and the camber strain is equal on all : in B excessive " toe out " throws extra strain on the offside front tyre, while in C excessive " toe in " is straining the nearside front tyre.

wheels seldom wear unevenly. Irregular wear usually takes the form of a series of depressions or " scollops " in the tread pattern, at about twenty places around the circumference. When a car habitually, and incurably, wears out its front tyres unevenly, the owner should change the wheels round with reasonable frequency.

Under-inflation is a cause of irregular wear, through the increased flexing of the carcase of the cover, which results in the tread segments " shuffling " on the road and, in consequence, wearing more rapidly. It is also a fact that under-inflation (below the recommended pressure) reduces the capacity of the tyre to generate cornering force ; in other words, lowers its " cornering power." A test made under carefully controlled conditions (in which pressure was the only variable) showed that ten per cent. reduced pressure increased the rate of tread wear by thirteen per cent. Regular attention to tyre pressure should be paid *when the tyres are cold*, and one of the most effective methods of prolonging tyre life is to change the wheels from one position on the car to another about every 2,000 miles, so that the wearing tendency is not continuously in the same direction.

Some Queries to Ask Yourself at this Point

1.—Describe briefly the various components in the transmission of power from engine to road wheels.
2.—Describe the basic construction of (*a*) a normal friction clutch and (*b*) a fluid flywheel.
3.—What is a dog clutch, and where is it employed in the transmission ?
4.—What is the meaning of synchro-mesh ?
5.—For what reason is a universal joint employed, and where ? Describe one form of such joint.

6.—What are the two principal types of drive used in the back axle and of what order would the final drive ratio be ?

7.—Give an outline of the necessity for a differential, and a description of its basic principle.

8.—How should a driver set his controls when " coasting " ? And what should *never* be done to arrive at the same effect ?

9.—Why might the sparking plugs soot up if a hill were being descended with the gearbox in use as an auxiliary brake ?

10.—How would you re-engage top gear after descending a hill with the gear in neutral ?

11.—Describe some of the forms of springing used on a car.

12.—For what reason is a shock absorber fitted ?

13.—What is understood by the word " servo " as applied to a braking system ?

14.—Describe briefly the general lay-out of a steering gear.

15.—What is meant by the terms " toe in " and " toe out " ? What is the component that governs them ?

16.—Explain how tyre-wear is intensified through driving technique.

17.—If tyres wear unevenly, what is the trouble likely to be caused by, and how can it best be overcome ?

PART III

MAINTENANCE

WHILE this book is not intended to be a highly technical manual for the motorist who desires to undertake thorough overhauls of every major part of his car—and for which purpose many excellent works are available—it is as well that a newcomer to the ranks of car-owners should appreciate that there are certain tasks which it will pay him to attend to personally. I propose, therefore, to give a general description of those that could be classed as maintenance and running repairs, also some remarks about the more major upkeep jobs.

One of the first things that almost every prospective motorist says, when the intention of purchasing the first car is being discussed, is : " But what should I do if the car broke down miles from anywhere ? " Well, the best answer to that is to become familiar with the reason for each working part and the quota it contributes to the whole—the whole being understood to mean a properly-running car. If the reader has conscientiously absorbed what has been written in the previous sections of this book, he (or she) will by now have a reasonably clear impression of what causes the wheels to go round. This knowledge, applied logically, ought to provide an answer to almost any untoward incident that may occur on the road. Let us take an example at random.

You are travelling along when the car comes to an abrupt halt—the engine has simply died. What is the cause ? The petrol gauge shows that the tank is not empty (or, if no gauge, a dipstick reveals some fuel still in hand).

Running over the essentials, we realise that, so long as there is petrol passing into the carburettor, and out of it into the induction pipe in gasified form, and so long as the engine is drawing it in and the valves working properly, the trouble must lie in failure on the part of the electrical system, whereby the spark is not occurring at the plug points. Now to check.

First, if the ignition warning lamp lights, and the starter works, the battery must be supplying sufficient power to operate the ignition. Second, if examination of the carburettor shows that there is petrol in the float chamber, the fuel pump and the pipe line from the tank must be in order. Third, if petrol starts to drip from the carburettor when the hand-priming lever on it is operated, the jet cannot be completely stopped up. Fourth, if a spark is seen to jump from the end of one of the high-tension leads when detached from the plug and held a short distance away from it, and the engine turned by means of the handle or starter, the ignition system is still working properly.

If all those points are checked through and found to be fully in order, the trouble would lie in some obscure matter such as a faulty coil, which appeared to give an ignition spark but which only gave it under test conditions, and not when the compression of the engine was adding to the load so that the defective coil could not overcome it. Or there might be a crack in the distributor casing, which would have a similar effect. These are, however, infrequent causes of breakdown with a car which is in reasonably good condition.

The majority of roadside difficulties arise from one or other of the following causes :—

1.—Lack of petrol in the tank.

2.—Dirt or water in the tank, and drawn into the pipe line when the level in the tank gets low.

3.—An air-lock in the pipe line, or a clogging of it by water or dirt.

4.—Dirt or water in the fuel pump or in the carburettor.

5.—Blocking of the carburettor jet by grit.

6.—Ignition failure through a wire jumping off a terminal on coil or distributor, or a high-tension lead coming detached (this would cause only the plug affected to cease work).

7.—A defect occurring inside the coil.

8.—A defect occurring inside the distributor.

9.—A fracture having occurred at some point in the wiring of the car.

10.—Faulty plug(s).

11.—A sticking valve.

12.—Broken valve spring, causing a valve to operate erratically.

These are all separate and distinct from major engine troubles, which obviously cannot be rectified by the roadside. The faculty that the motorist gradually develops, mainly by experience but largely by instinctive realisation of what is going on (or should be going on) inside his engine, helps him to lay a finger on most troubles when, and if, they occur.

By this I mean that there are usually symptoms which convey a fairly accurate idea of where trouble has arisen. For instance, if an engine stops firing with complete suddenness the cause is almost certainly in the ignition system. If it coughs and spits itself to a standstill, then the reason lies somewhere in the petrol and induction system. If the engine makes unpleasant mechanical noises before stopping, then the trouble is something serious internally.

Every motorist must devote a certain amount of personal attention to his car if he desires to maintain it in the most efficient and most economical condition. Depending on how far he drives it, he should, either weekly or every few hundred miles, check on the following items :—

Sufficiency of water in the radiator.

Oil in sump sufficiently high up the dipstick to be well above low-level mark.

Tyres at correct pressure.

Plates in battery not above level of electrolyte.

The above are what may be termed the everyday routine points that demand attention if the car is to be operated efficiently, even though it may be practically new. If the radiator loses water, and the cause is obviously not boiling, the first thing to examine is the circulating pump (if one is fitted), for the gland which is fitted at the front end of the pump spindle to hold the water in the pump and prevent it leaking is apt to require occasional tightening up, or even re-packing. The usual principle is that a strip of prepared string is wound around the spindle, and is compressed by an adjustable nut ; this constitutes the " packing gland," and wear is liable to reduce the bulk of the string so that the nut must be tightened to take up the slack.

Another point where leaks may occur is at the junction between rubber hose connections and the metal water pipes. Rubber hose is called for owing to the necessity of having a flexible connection between engine and radiator, since most engines are nowadays mounted on rubber pads to absorb vibration before it can pass to the chassis and body. The rubber hose connections are generally made tight on the metal portions by a clip which is provided with a screw-up adjustment. Unless kept tight, these allow globules of water to escape, often in an almost unnoticeable way, and, after the car has been left standing for a time, the level of water in the radiator may have fallen considerably, with the result that the engine boils. When this occurs, remove the radiator filler cap with very great caution, since the steam pressure inside the radiator will possibly blow it off the last thread, and boiling water may gush forth in a cascade. It is advisable not to fill up with cold water immediately, for the cylinder block around the valve ports may be red hot.

It is a good practice now and again to drain the water out of the radiator and to refill with fresh, especially if a supply of soft water is available, as this obviates the formation of too much lime inside the radiator gills and pipes. A radiator consists of long passages with a thin metal covering ; the thinner the metal, the more effective is the radiator, for, after all, its function is to dissipate the heat taken from the engine by the water. Hence, any serious quantity of lime formed inside the radiator will reduce its cooling properties, just as it makes the domestic kettle boil more slowly.

In cold weather, frost will first of all nip the lower part of the radiator, where the water stays cold longest. When starting off on a bitter morning, therefore, mask the *bottom* of the radiator with rug, newspaper or some other protection. Leave the top uncovered (unless a proper radiator muff is fitted), but remember that the first heat generated by the engine will pass to the upper part of the radiator through the medium of the water, while there may even be ice in the lowest part of it. Although this ice may not burst the pipe (if you are lucky), it can quite easily seal off the outlet at the bottom of the radiator when the engine will boil merrily in a very short time.

Many motorists who have to use their cars in all weathers

fill up with anti-freeze at the beginning of the winter, and, provided a good brand is used, there will be no harm caused to the engine. The effect of anti-freeze liquid added to the radiator's contents is that the freezing point is lowered, the amount by which it is lowered depending on the nature of the compound employed and the quantity put into the water. The recommended quantity will vary according to the normal temperatures likely to be encountered in any given country or district, and this recommendation must be given careful attention, for what may be quite satisfactory in, say, southern England may not be adequate for the lowest temperatures experienced in the Highlands of Scotland. Use only good brands of anti-freeze, as cheaper kinds may cause trouble with water leakage around the rubber hose connections due to deposit of slimy substance at the joints.

If anti-freeze is not put in the radiator, it will be necessary, when frost threatens, to drain the water out of the entire engine, that is, from the cylinder jackets as well as from the radiator and pipes. Usually there is a drain plug or tap provided at the lowest part of the circulation system for this purpose. If through frost precautions being inadequate a fracture of the cylinder block does occur, the owner should be very careful to entrust the work of repair to a firm specialising in welding processes, as an incompetent repairer may spoil the block irreparably whereas the expert would have made a serviceable job of it.

The amount of oil in the sump is not important provided it is above the low-level mark on the dipstick and *not above the high-level mark*. In the latter case, a surplus of oil is very liable to cause " flooding " of the base chamber and, when that does occur, fouling of the sparking plugs and valves is the probable aftermath. A little topping-up at

F

fairly frequent intervals is the best procedure to adopt, and the oil should always be given ample time to settle down and drain into the base chamber before reading its level on the dipstick; it is best to do this when the engine is warm.

A thing to bear in mind about the engine lubricating oil is that it acts as part of the cooling system, for, as we have seen, it is the oil splashing about inside the pistons which draws from that part of them heat which the cooling water can never approach. Therefore, it is as well to keep the level of oil in the sump in proximity to the high mark, because the greater the quantity, obviously the greater the cooling capacity. And the sump should be drained with regularity and comparative frequency; you will lose nothing except the cost of the oil, and you may gain far more than that in the service and longevity that you receive from the engine.

Many people enquire about the value or utility of upper cylinder lubricants and petrol additives. The general answer is that, if of reputable make, they will do no harm and may do a considerable amount of good. When a suitable lubricant of this nature is added to the petrol in the tank, and mixes with it, a certain degree of oiliness is imparted to the explosive charge as it enters the engine through the induction ports. This has the effect of imparting some much-needed lubrication to the stem of the inlet valve, which otherwise works in a dry condition. But here, again, sufficient is enough; in other words, an excess of oil on the valve stem may cause it to stick and work erratically just as dryness might do the same.

Once inside the engine, upper cylinder lubricant does find its way to just that zone indicated by the title—to the top end of the cylinder above the piston rings where oil from the base chamber is almost unknown. How desirable it is to have some lubricant here is realised when a worn engine is dismantled; measurement of the top portion of the cylinder bore may reveal anything up to ten times as much wear as there is at the bottom end. Although this wear may not be caused by friction from the piston (much of it is due to corrosion arising from the " wet " gas in a cold engine) at least a film of oil deposited by upper cylinder lubricant may have a beneficial effect.

There are other additives which are recommended for use in the sump, and even the gearbox and back axle. These consist of a comparatively thin, but specially compounded oil, which is mixed with the normal lubricant in the components mentioned and have the result of reducing friction. As a result, an engine will run more freely and at a lower temperature than when running on the normal brand of oil exclusively. Petrol consumption is thereby improved, likewise acceleration and even maximum speed. I have personally conducted tests over considerable distances with at least one such additive, and have certainly enjoyed the benefits claimed.

As regards tyre pressures, the earlier remarks on this subject leave little to be added on the subject of the importance of adhering to recommended pressures. A gauge ought to be carried by every motorist, so that he may check pressures readily without having to take the car to a garage for the purpose. And do not forget to keep the spare wheel's tyre up to the right pressure. When changing the wheels round in order to even up wear on all the tyres, it is best to make a chalk mark before removing them from the car to identify the position from which each one came. Even though it may be possible to jack up only one wheel at a time, it is surprising how easily confusion can arise before the whole job is completed. Three suggestions for changing round are given in the diagram.

The battery is a most important component, and ought to receive more attention than it normally gets. All too frequently the car-maker has placed it in an inaccessible spot, but out of sight, out of mind is a short-term policy. The liquid (" electrolyte ") in the battery should always be covering the tops of the plates, although often a piece of mirror has to be held over the vent hole, periscope fashion, in order to ascertain the position within. Also, to introduce distilled water for topping-up may involve the use of a cranked spout which will pour round a corner ; a recently introduced gadget for this purpose has an ingenious device which allows only the correct level to be reached when the water flows in.

Keep a close watch, too, on the terminals of the battery. They grow a white fungus (" sulphate ") on the least provocation, and the only way to prevent this is to keep the terminals well greased. Once the sulphating has set in, it may eat through the lead on the terminal post if too long neglected, with results that can prove unpleasant or even disastrous.

At somewhat longer intervals than the foregoing, further items require attention. There are maintenance matters to attend to which include the following :—

Brake adjustment or renovation.
Clutch ditto.
Attention to gearbox and back axle.
Cleaning out petrol system.
Decarbonising engine and general tuning up.

The braking system on a modern car is not to be " played about " with unless he who does so is possessed of reasonably good understanding of the exact procedure. With the increasing use of servo devices, a maladjustment may prove serious because it will throw the entire balancing plan out of gear. It must be remembered that exactly the same pressure must be imposed on the brakes on opposite sides of the car, or a pull one way or the other will be set up which may send the car off at a tangent when an emergency application is made on a treacherous road surface.

Therefore, no work should be done by an unskilled owner to his brakes over and above what he is told he may do in the car manufacturer's handbook. Most braking systems are of proprietary make, and it is good policy to call in their service stations' specialised help when the brakes appear to need some attention. In the event of new linings being required for the brake shoes, it will usually be possible to arrange for reconditioned shoes to be fitted.

One point to which the owner should pay great attention when routine greasing of the chassis is being done is that an excess of lubricant in the front-wheel hubs should be scrupulously avoided. As we have seen, the major part of the braking effort is taken by the front-wheel brakes, in the course of which a certain amount of heat is bound to be generated. Even, therefore, though the wheel hubs are lubricated with grease, the effect of braking will be to thin this, when it will run almost as freely as oil. Centrifugal force will tend to distribute it outwards, and any surplus that may have been put into the hubs is prone to find its way on to the brake drums. The trouble which this can cause must be experienced to be believed—but it is better to remain in ignorance of it !

The clutch operating mechanism will tend to stretch after periods of use, and the driver will probably find that gear changing becomes more difficult, also he may not be able to engage bottom gear, with the car stationary and engine running, without making a grating noise. Examination of the withdrawal mechanism will usually reveal the adjustment necessary to give the clutch pedal back its proper amount of travel, but when making the adjustment care is necessary to prevent the clutch pedal losing its requisite degree of slackness before taking the load. Without a slight amount of " lost motion " in the pedal there will be a tendency for the clutch to develop a permanent slip.

The gearbox and back axle call for very little attention, although it is desirable to verify the state of their lubrication at intervals and occasionally to drain and refill them. In both cases an excess of lubricant will be liable to cause trouble, for the clutch may suffer in the case of too much oil in the gearbox, while the rear-wheel brake drums will develop the same defects as those mentioned for the front wheels if the back axle has a surplus of oil in it.

I have already touched upon the trouble that arises from water getting into the petrol system. The greatest possible care should always be taken to see that no water finds its way into the petrol tank, for it is exceedingly difficult to clear every particle out once it is in. Erratic running, stopping, popping in the carburettor and generally unsatisfactory behaviour on the part of the engine can all arise from water finding its way first into the tank, then into the pipe line and finally into the carburettor. A lock to the cap of the tank filler is almost always worth while, because sometimes children (and others who should know better) think it a fine joke to pour some water in. Other practical jokers (!) are prone to insert lumps of sugar, which have a deleterious effect on petrol.

Once the tank is known to have water in it, every effort

should be made to drain it out. Unfortunately, the drain plug which most tanks have is not always situated in the right place to permit of this, and, when that is the case, there is no option but to have the tank removed from the chassis and thoroughly swilled out—with petrol, of course. Baffle plates are often fitted inside the tank to prevent an undue amount of " swishing about " on the part of the petrol, and these are a complication when the cleaning out process is in progress. Nevertheless, it is absolutely essential that no water be left remaining in the tank, or, for that matter, any rust. The latter is as big a nuisance as water.

The petrol pipe line can usually be cleared out by pumping air through it (the compressed air system which most garages have is useful in this connection). The petrol pump will also require thorough cleaning if the trouble is bad, likewise the carburettor, which has gauze filters that are rather liable to become choked and should be taken out regularly for inspection and cleaning. But, once you have experienced the annoyance that can be caused by water in the petrol system—and it always seems to come to a head on dark, wet nights or at the most inconvenient times— you will decide that the most comprehensive measures are worth while taking to rectify the matter.

The combustion taking place inside the engine naturally causes an amount of burnt matter to accumulate inside those parts where the greatest heat occurs. These are (a) the inside of the cylinder head, (b) the top of the piston and (c) the upper part of the side walls of the piston, including behind the piston rings. Lubricating oil which finds its way into these parts is charred by the burning gas, and deposits itself in the form of a hard carbon which eventually will become so thick that it curtails the space allowed for the compression and combustion of the gas.

The carbon also has the habit of glowing here and there, and this causes what is called pre-ignition of the compressed charge ; in other words, the glow forestalls the spark as a means of igniting the mixture and therefore makes the explosion occur prematurely, with the result that the engine develops an unpleasant knocking. The distance that an engine will run before having to be cleaned out internally varies with the type and the oil used, but it is safe to say that it will need doing at between 15,000 and 20,000 miles.

To decarbonise an engine it is necessary to dismantle all the connections to the cylinder block or cylinder head, and to remove one or other so that the pistons are exposed. On some engines the cylinder head is detachable separately from the cylinder block, while other designs have a one-piece cylinder and head. No precise instructions can therefore be given, but should be obtained from the manufacturers of the car concerned. In any event, to decarbonise an engine is not work that the amateur owner-driver would be inclined to tackle unless he had a certain amount of experience, since there are many unexpected " snags " that would make it necessary eventually to call in skilled assistance. Far better, therefore, to place the job in the hands of a good garage.

An engine which has run for a long distance—say 30,000 miles—will develop a tendency to consume considerable quantities of oil, some of which will be dissipated from the exhaust pipe in the form of blue smoke. (Do not confuse this with the black smoke that is caused by too rich a mixture, or the white steam which arises from moisture in the engine and exhaust system being vaporised on a cold morning when the car is first started up.) Clouds of blue smoke emanating from the exhaust pipe indicate that the cylinder bore has worn and that, in consequence, oil is finding its way past the pistons and rings into the combustion chamber.

The cure for cylinder wear is to have a reboring operation performed, when the diameter is increased by a certain amount—this may be anything up to, say, ten-thousandths of an inch or even more. The amount by which it is safe to bore out the cylinder depends, however, on the metal of which the cylinder block is made, and only an expert can determine this. When bored out, there are two alternatives as regards the pistons ; one is to have a larger set fitted to suit the increased diameter of the cylinder, the other is to have liners fitted in the cylinder, in which case the bore is not increased in its working size.

Cylinder linering is a process that is becoming more popular, especially where the engine is expected to give considerable further service. Cylinder liners are to be had in hard metal, while some of the best are of steel, chromium-plated, and, once these are fitted, the cylinders will probably never again have to be attended to on account of wear. Naturally, the cost of the liners must be taken into consideration, but, where big mileages are covered, they may prove to be an economy as compared with fitting a complete new set of pistons. The decision must, of course, rest with the owner of the car.

Another device whereby increased wear is obtained from cylinder bores is the chromium-plated piston ring. One of these is fitted in the topmost groove in each piston, and has the effect of minimising the " shearing " action of the ring on the cast-iron cylinder bore. A word of advice is, however, important here : If you fit a chromium-plated piston ring do not also fit a chromium-plated cylinder liner, for chromium does not take kindly to working on itself, and seizing-up will ensue. Use, therefore, a chromium-plated piston ring only in a cast-iron cylinder or liner, and vice versa.

The virtues of chromium as a wear-resisting metal for the inside of a motor-engine are becoming more and more appreciated, and certain manufacturers finish off the cylinder bores with a plating of chromium. It is, however, an expensive and a somewhat " tricky " process, since this metal is one that refuses to carry a coating of oil unless special arrangements are made, and, as we have seen, a film of oil in the cylinder bore is an absolute necessity. At the same time, when the plating process is properly carried out, the results are excellent, as chromium is also a prime resister of corrosion. Cylinders fitted with steel liners chromium-plated have been known to run for fully a quarter of a million miles without there being any need for reboring, or, in fact, any serious wear.

Some Questions to Ask Yourself at this Point

1.—Run through the various processes which cause a motor car engine to work, beginning with the petrol in the tank.
2.—Mention some of the reasons why an engine might cease to function.
3.—Where would you look first for the cause of (a) the engine stopping abruptly, and (b) spluttering to a standstill ?
4.—What are the four most important items to check over either weekly or every few hundred miles ?
5.—Enumerate some of the points where the radiator may suffer loss of water.
6.—Where would you expect frosty weather to cause trouble in the water circulating system when the car

is being driven for the first few miles, i.e., before it has become warmed up ?

7.—Why should the engine sump not be filled above the high-level mark on the dipstick ?

8.—What is meant by the term " upper cylinder lubricant " ?

9.—With what should the liquid contents of the battery be " topped-up " ?

10.—What is the name for the white fungus which appears on the terminals of a neglected battery ?

11.—Why should an excess of lubricant in the wheel-hub bearings be avoided ?

12.—If water should find its way into the petrol tank, what would you expect the result to be upon the running of the engine ?

13.—How does carbon form inside the cylinder, and what effect can it have upon the running of the engine ?

14.—At approximately what period does an engine require to be decarbonised ?

15.—Why does a worn engine consume a greater quantity of lubricating oil than is normal ?

16.—What would you expect to be the cause of smoke of the following colour being emitted from the exhaust pipe : (a) blue, (b) black ?

17.—What is the cure for a worn cylinder bore ?

18.—Describe two methods whereby the tendency on the part of cylinder bores to wear may be minimised.

PART IV

ON THE ROAD

BEFORE any person is eligible to be in charge of a mechanically-propelled vehicle on the public highway he or she must be in possession of a driving licence. In order to ensure, so far as is practicable, that only those competent in handling the controls and acquainted with the code of behaviour governing every road user shall be issued with a full driving licence, a driving test has to be passed under the supervision of an official examiner.

The first step towards the passing of the test is for the novice to obtain a provisional driving licence, which is done by filling up form D.L.1 (available at any Post Office) and, after duly completing it, to forward it accompanied by 5s. to the Taxation Department of the county or county borough in which the applicant resides. The provisional licence, which must be signed immediately on receipt, is available for three months and can be renewed as often as desired on payment of further 5s. fees.

A provisional driving licence entitles the holder to drive a car on the public roads provided it displays at the front and rear official " L " plates and carries an experienced driver (one who has held a full licence for at least two years). The car must, of course, be taxed and insured against third party risks.

The novice driver is thus enabled to gain familiarity with both the controls of the car and road conditions in general. Concurrently, he will be well advised to study the Highway Code seriously, bearing in mind that this is not a book of instruction, but a book of rules based on the fundamentals of good driving. To grasp the principle behind the rulings of the Code will enable satisfactory replies to be given to an examiner's questions when the driving test is taken, even though the replies may not be word for word the same as printed in the book.

When it is considered that the time has come for taking the test, form D.L.26 should be obtained, completed and forwarded with 7s. 6d. to the Supervising Examiner of the area in which the applicant lives (a list is printed on the back of the form). An appointment will be made and the date, time and place notified. In keeping the appointment, it is important that the provisional driving licence should be taken along for the examiner's inspection, also the certificate of insurance.

The course over which the test is to be made will have been selected to include a variety of traffic conditions, but it is a mistake to believe that the person being tested will be called upon to perform any " freak " driving or tricks to demonstrate outstanding cleverness. All that is required is to satisfy the examiner that the car is under complete control in the driver's hands, and that he can handle it with safety on the prescribed route and also carry out certain everyday manœuvres, such as reversing. The duration of the test is about half-an-hour.

The following list indicates the nature of the test and the particular things the driver will be asked to do :—

1.—To start up the engine and to drive the car in a forward direction, using each intermediate gear and eventually reaching top.

2.—To give the authorised signals, using the hand until such time as the examiner gives permission for mechanical signals to be employed (providing the car is equipped with them).

3.—To conform with traffic control signals, whether given by lights or by police constables.

4.—To make turnings to right or left as instructed, and to negotiate road junctions or roundabouts as necessary.

5.—To understand authorised road signs and to conform with them.

6.—To overtake other vehicles whether moving or stationary, with proper caution and giving the appropriate signals.

7.—To make a right-hand turn out of a main road, across the oncoming traffic stream. To make a left-hand turn.

8.—To make (a) a normal stop and (b) an emergency stop.

9.—To set the car in motion on an upgrade without slipping back.

10.—To turn the car round in the width of the roadway, using reverse.

11.—To reverse into a narrow opening at right-angles to the road on which the car is standing.

12.—To demonstrate general control of the car by reliable steering and smooth gear-changing and braking as and when necessary.

13.—To be able to answer satisfactorily questions having a bearing on the Highway Code.

It may be useful to mention a few points to which a novice, during the course of his practising for the test, should pay special attention, as the more instinctively they come the greater will be the chances of performing well under the nervous strain of the examination.

First, get yourself comfortably seated and see that all the doors are properly closed. Next, always verify that the gear lever is in neutral before switching on the ignition, and see that the handbrake lever is on. Never touch the gear lever without previously pressing out the clutch pedal (provided the car is of normal control, i.e., not with pre-selector gearbox).

Do not race the engine unduly when letting in the clutch; at the same time, do not let the engine stall because it is turning over too slowly to take the load.

Take a glance in the rear mirror before setting the car in motion to verify that no other vehicle is coming up behind. In any case, give the hand signal (" I am going to turn to my right ") before actually getting under way.

Do not make the mistake of " dwelling " in bottom gear too long—get into second as soon as the speedometer shows eight to ten m.p.h. Use top gear as much as possible (without " hanging-on " too long and letting the engine labour), and try to maintain a road speed under normal traffic conditions of twenty-five to twenty-eight m.p.h. Glance at the speedometer every now and again to make certain that it never shows above thirty m.p.h. while in a restricted area.

When slowing down for traffic, demonstrate your control of the gears by changing to the next lower gear in order to accelerate better when the road clears; do not give the examiner the impression that you are shy of using the gear lever.

Never forget to look in the rear mirror and give the hand signal when pulling out or starting from rest, even though the road behind may be clear. Always give the hand signal (" I am slowing down ") in good time before stopping, except in emergency.

If using mechanical trafficators, always listen for them to cancel themselves after the turn is made (if of the self-cancelling type). Acquire the habit of glancing at the control now and again to see that it has returned to normal.

When turning to the right out of a main road, first give the appropriate signal and then gradually edge the car to the centre line of the road. If oncoming traffic compels you to stop, do so at a position which is in line with *your* traffic line in the road you are going to enter—in other words, take the turn wide so that any vehicle coming in the other direction will have plenty of room. Proceed to make the turn as soon as traffic permits, but, above all, don't cut the corner.

When turning to the left do not get too close to the near-side kerb or you may foul the angle at the bend. On the other hand, do not swing out so far in the road as to impede vehicles coming up behind, and which are going straight on.

To turn the car round in the width of the road, first look in the rear mirror and give the hand signal, then drive the car forward on the right lock. Just before reaching the opposite kerb slow the car down to a mere crawl and quickly lock the wheels over the other way. Stop the car before the wheels foul the kerb and put the hand brake on. Engage reverse gear, take off the brake and go backwards on the left lock, repeating the previous procedure with the wheels before the car can touch the kerb, and again put the hand-brake on to hold the car. Engage first gear and run forward on the right lock, when the car should complete the turn without fouling the nearside kerb. The object of putting on the handbrake each time is that, if the manœuvre were called for on a road without kerbs, the car might run into the ditch—a point watched by examiners.

When making an emergency stop, give no signal but merely press hard on the clutch and brake pedals simultaneously. If practising this, see that the road behind is clear : if ordered to do so in the driving test, it will be assumed that the examiner has himself verified it. Never touch the gear lever until the car has come to rest. When making a normal stop, give the hand signal and gently apply the footbrake. The clutch pedal should be pressed out just before the car comes to rest, and the gear lever put into neutral as soon as it has done so. The hand brake should be applied before taking the foot from the brake pedal.

When overtaking other vehicles be quite certain that the road is clear ahead for a fully adequate distance and that there are no side turnings from which other traffic might emerge. Remember that the fundamental principle is that the driver of an overtaking vehicle is responsible for doing so without endangering other road users or causing them to have to change direction or speed appreciably. The hand signal must be given (" I am going to turn right ") after first glancing in the rear mirror and making sure that nobody is already on your tail. Once you have made the decision to overtake, carry out the operation without hesitation or drawing back at the last moment, but do not make the decision unless you are positive that you can do it.

There are some strict injunctions given in the Highway Code as to when it is unsafe to overtake, and these should be very carefully memorised and obeyed.

The meaning of traffic-light signals should be thoroughly understood. Red means *stop* and wait behind the stop line on the road surface. Red with amber means *stop*, but be prepared to go when the green shows. Green means proceed if the road is clear, but with particular care if turning either to right or left. If the former, traffic coming straight across towards you has priority; if turning to the left, beware of pedestrians crossing. Amber alone means *stop* at the stop line unless, when amber appears, you have already crossed the stop line or are so close to it that to pull up might cause an accident. A green arrow shown with the red signal allows vehicles to proceed (or " filter ") in the direction indicated by the arrow.

White lines on the road surface are for the guidance of road users and should be respected as directions to assist in the safe and orderly flow of traffic. (White lines include yellow lines and studs.) A broken line along the centre of the road is to divide traffic lanes, and where the line is solid very great care is necessary. It is a technical offence to overtake a moving vehicle, or to park your own, where there is a solid line.

Road signs are of three types—prohibitory, mandatory and warning or informative. The first, as their name implies, prohibit passage, either to all vehicles or to some, or forbid parking. These signs are circular in shape or are surmounted with a solid red disc. Mandatory signs convey a message requiring traffic to follow a certain route, or to halt; these are provided with a red ring and/or a triangle, the latter being inverted. Warning and informative signs are designed to convey some special message as to road conditions, and are usually surmounted with a red triangle, not inverted.

To all candidates who seriously desire to pass their driving tests at the first attempt it is recommended that a trial run be made beforehand in the company of an experienced instructor who knows the details of official procedure. He would assume the role of the examiner on this run but would have the advantage of being able to tell the candidate where his driving was weak and where additional practice would be beneficial. Many candidates have been instructed by friends, who may themselves be good and experienced drivers, but who are not conversant with the methods that are officially regarded as being the correct one. Those who may be classed as veterans, having taught themselves or " picked it up " twenty or thirty years ago, had the advantage of learning when traffic conditions were very different from what they are to-day, and in any case they have acquired over a lengthy period a degree of competence that cannot possibly be expected of a novice under present circumstances.

In the event of failing the test the examiner will give the unsuccessful candidate a printed form (D.L.24), which has details of the test printed on it, and will mark the particular items in respect of which he considered the required standard was not reached. There is no limit to the number of tests that may be taken, the fee being 7s. 6d. each time, but a period of not less than one calendar month must elapse between them. Similarly, there is no limit to the number of provisional licences that may be taken out after the previous one has expired.

To those who pass the test, the examiner hands a pink certificate which must be sent, with the provisional licence, to the authority by which the latter was issued. The licence will be returned with the provisional restrictions officially cancelled and it may then be used as a full licence during the unexpired period for which it was issued. A full licence is valid for one year from date of issue, and costs 5s.

Insurance

The private motorist must insure against third party personal injury risks, so that he can be in a position to pay compensation for any injury that he may cause to other people. The claimant may be a pedestrian or any person, even a passenger in the car against which liability is alleged. This insurance is a legal liability upon every owner of a vehicle that is mechanically propelled, and a certificate to prove that the insurance is in effect has to be produced whenever a road fund licence is applied for.

Third party insurance does not cover the cost of making good damage to a motorist's own car ; this is only covered by a policy known as " Comprehensive," which naturally costs a good deal more than mere Third Party. There are, however, many modifications possible with full comprehensive insurance which can effect its cost considerably. You may, for instance, obtain a reduction in premium by limiting use of the car to one named driver, or by undertaking to defray the first £5 or £10 of any claim. Again, there will probably be a " No Claim " bonus at the end of an accident-free year. Extra premium will be demanded where the car is mainly used in areas of heavy traffic, such as the big cities, or additional insurance in the form of personal accident, moral liability to passengers, and other desired cover.

It is a mistake for any car owner to economise by taking out a policy with a " cheap " company, which may offer a few shillings off the premium but will be unsatisfactory when the time comes for a claim to be made. It will then, perhaps, be found that there is some restrictive clause which throws an unexpected onus on the motorist and may cause serious embarrassment when he believed himself to be comprehensively insured.

If a motorist is involved in an accident causing injury to a human being or domestic animal (the term excludes cats and poultry), he must stop and give his name and address to any person who, with reasonable cause, asks for it. If, for any reason, he does not do so, he must report the accident to a police station or to a police officer within twenty-four hours. A motorist should always carry his driving licence and insurance certificate on his person, as he will be required to produce them to a constable on the spot, or have to take them to a police station later.

Where personal injury to a third party necessitates immediate medical or surgical attention, the car owner is held responsible for payment of 12s. 6d. in fees to the medical practitioner or the hospital in respect of each person treated. This liability is placed on the owner of the vehicle irrespective of whether the driver was at fault, and is usually paid by the insurance company, but does not count as a claim. A report of any accident should be sent to the motorist's insurance company, together with the names and addresses of at least two witnesses, if obtainable, with the least possible delay. Most comprehensive insurance policies cover the cost of towage of a damaged vehicle to the premises of the nearest competent repairer.

The Motoring Organisations

A very large proportion of motorists belong to one or other of the two motoring organisations, the Automobile Association and the Royal Automobile Club. They are familiarly known, respectively, as the "A.A." and the " R.A.C." Both offer similar services although the R.A.C., being the recognised national club so far as sporting events are concerned, has responsibilities in this field which are not shared by the A.A. The two organisations work together very amicably and certain of their services to the motorist are pooled—this applies to their hotel recommendations and to their telephone boxes at numerous points along the roadside.

The patrols are a familiar sight on roads throughout England, Scotland and Wales, and these men, who are usually mounted on motor cycle and sidecar combinations, are available to render assistance to members carrying the organisation's badge. They are able to effect minor repairs and are trained in first-aid. In the event of a member having trouble with the police, the organisations provide him with free legal aid, either as to advice or defence. They offer also a free breakdown service which includes mechanical first-aid, delivery of oil or petrol, changing a wheel, or towage.

In the matter of touring, whether at home or abroad, both the A.A. and the R.A.C. maintain very efficient departments which will provide recommended routes and also the documents necessary to the taking of a car to other countries. They keep a staff of officers at the ports where cars are shipped, and facilitate the passage of touring motorists through the Customs on both sides of the Channel. They issue handbooks which contain details of hotels they have appointed after careful inspection, also garages, up and down the country, and in certain foreign countries visited by their members.

The technical departments will furnish free advice to members, and will inspect and report upon the condition of used cars at moderate fees. They maintain a recovery service for insurance claims, which negotiates with insurers and other parties with a view to the settlement of claims without litigation. They have a number of branch offices in provincial centres to expedite the handling of their services.

In the case of the A.A., breakdown vehicles are in operation during the night in London and Birmingham, controlled by radio from headquarters, so that a motorist needing assistance has only to ring through to the office and state where his car is stranded ; the nearest vehicle will then be guided by instructions sent out over special short-wave radio.

The R.A.C., as the governing body in motor sport in Great Britain, has the task of organising important races and trials, and also supervises the sporting events held by all other clubs in the country. The R.A.C. has two types of membership, one entitling use of the clubhouses in Pall Mall, London, and at Woodcote Park, Epsom. The other (associate membership) confers the various privileges set out above with the exception of use of the clubhouses, and, like A.A. membership, costs the motorist the moderate subscription of £2 2s. 0d. per annum.

Some motorists like to join a local automobile club for social or sporting reasons, and there are many such throughout the country. All recognised clubs are affiliated to the R.A.C., and membership of them automatically makes a motorist an associate member of the parent body and entitled to its benefits. The addresses of affiliated clubs, with name of the secretary, are obtainable from the R.A.C., at 83 Pall Mall, London, S.W.1.

There are also other organisations catering for motorists which are not " recognised " clubs and do not carry the advantages of association with the R.A.C. Before joining, therefore, the motorist would be advised to ascertain exactly what benefits he will receive for his subscription. Sometimes they amount to no more than the right to display a badge on the car.

Conclusion

The fact that you are reading this book indicates that you are desirous of learning as much as possible about motoring and not content merely to pick it up as you go along. No book can teach a person *all* about motoring, for practice and experience alone can give a driver automatic and instinctive response to emergency happenings. It is based on intimate knowledge of the location of each control pedal or lever on any particular car and the exact degree in which it will function.

At least, however, a book can indicate how a good motorist should make his car behave in relation to the conditions ruling on the roads to-day. The essence of good manners is to be considerate of your neighbour, and that unspeakable fellow the roadhog can be just as much of a nuisance (and danger) whether at the wheel of a fiery sports car or a crawling small saloon. The " week-end driver " who ambles along the crown of a busy main road and dares other people to overtake him—*if they can*—is not thoroughly selfish but a real roadhog into the bargain.

A good driver is not necessarily a slow driver, but he will be a careful driver in that his car's speed will be adjusted whenever visibility or potential danger demand a reduction, and he will know his controls so thoroughly that reaction to any emergency is practically instantaneous—and effective. He seldom experiences what are known as " phenomenal avoidances " because he senses in advance that another driver, or a pedestrian, has the intention of doing something odd.

To drive in a spirit of competition upon the public highway is a reprehensible thing, and the cause of many an accident. If a car overtakes you, don't take it as an insult and set off in a do-or-die attempt to show its driver a thing or two. Keep turning a periodical eye on your rear mirror, and, if you notice a car coming up behind you at a speed faster than you are inclined to go yourself, draw over and signal its driver to pass. He may be in a hurry, and not merely anxious to demonstrate his car's superior speed.

But do, at all times, keep in mind the principles laid down in the Highway Code. Set a good example and demonstrate that you are upholding the fellowship of the road, the same type of camaraderie which once induced a motorist to stop and offer help to a comrade in distress. By so doing, you will be playing your part in promoting one of the most urgent needs of our age, the making of roads safer for all who use them.

INDEX

171